Welcom

CW00411510

By Ne

Welcome Aboard!

INTRODUCTION:

Welcome Aboard! And welcome to the ultimate insider's guide to planes and flying. Like most cabin crew I've flown thousands of passengers to hundreds of destinations – and I've learned a heck of a lot about planes, about people and about everything that goes bump in the night up at 35,000 feet.

Over the years I've also found that people are always full of questions for cabin crew. It's a secret world up there. And people want to know more about it. So here, in my first book, I've tried to answer as many of those questions as possible. I've included the serious ones, the funny ones and the downright weird ones we always seem to get asked mid-Atlantic.

I've divided it all up into four broad chapters. But in each section I've mixed things up so some of the answers are quite long, and others are short-haul and punchy. Some are really serious – the answers could save your life or the lives of those around you if it all kicks off. Others might just give some useful reassurance if you're a nervous flyer and want to know more about what's going on around you. And a whole lot of the questions are just a bit of fun. I want them to open the galley curtains and explain exactly what your cabin crew are likely to be doing or thinking at any given time during a flight.

And I'm always up for more so do get in touch. When I'm not collecting rubbish in a metal tube at 35,000 feet I'm aiming to go on to Twitter @WelcomeFlyers so send me a tweet if you've got any other questions you want an answer for or if you've got any quick facts or travel tips that you want to pass on to other flyers. I'll keep on updating *Welcome Aboard!* with new facts and info all the time.

Or just tweet me if you've got any other stories to tell the world about your dream trip – or your flight from hell.

And wherever you're going and whoever you're flying with – have a safe and happy flight!

CHAPTER ONE – For Your Comfort and Convenience.

*Flirting to get upgrades – Lying to get upgrades – Are you Bob? –
Doors to Automatic and Cross-Check – Mice on a plane – Snakes on
a plane – Wi-Fi in the air – Running out of chicken – Loud 'bongs'
before take-off – All the other 'bongs' – The sound of sawing wood –
Why we still have ashtrays – Upgrading vegetarians (why it doesn't
happen) – Getting downgraded – The Mad Man – Noisy airplane
toilets – Getting your bags – Changing nappies – Your in-flight meal
– Getting a decent drink – Running to the loo – Long and short haul
flights – First class catering – Bare feet in the toilet – Losing your
luggage – Who gets the armrest – Luxury in the pointy end of the
plane – Meanwhile in economy – Flying at 35,000 feet – Are we
moving yet - Changing seats in half-empty planes – Where does all
the rubbish go - What happens to all the champagne?*

CAN I FLIRT MY WAY TO AN UPGRADE?

You can try. And your crew will love you for it. A bit of flirting from
passengers can get us through the longest of flights. Outrageous
compliments are very welcome. Pure, naked flattery is wonderful.
But will any of it get you moved into a big, fat seat at the pointy end
of the plane? I think I'm going to have to say no.

It's the same for the people who swear that it pays to dress
smartly for the airport check-in desk in the hope of getting
upgraded. People still talk about this supposedly magic code called
SFU or 'Suitable for Upgrade' that can get tapped into your file at
check-in if you act super-polite, wear a tie or generally look ready

6

for business. But SFU doesn't exist anymore – and ground crew friends say it never really did.

Upgrades do exist, of course. They're given out every day, sometimes on every flight. But in today's world they're handed out by computers. Modern airlines are run by accountants. It's all about the bottom line. They want to maximise profits or minimise losses – and one way to do that is to keep loyal customers happy. Sign up to your airline's frequent flyer scheme and they'll be able to track where and when you fly – and how much you pay for your ticket. They can track the trends: are you starting to spend more, or less than you were a year ago? Are you flying on rival airlines in the same alliance more than you were? Do you deserve a pat on the back for staying loyal, or a nudge to keep you that way in the future?

If the algorithms devised by the computer teams suggest that you need some travel TLC, then you get the upgrade, regardless of what you're wearing or how often you compliment the cabin crew on their hair.

Best advice? Always sign up for as many frequent flyer schemes as you can. If you're not in, you're not going to win that upgrade. It might take many flights to get your membership noticed by the all-powerful computer. But then again it might not. Airlines sometimes do special offers for new scheme members – new customers got instant upgrades on one American airline a few years ago. On some routes you may also find that even a modest pile of air miles makes you the 'richest' passenger on the plane. So if upgrades are on offer then one of them might come your way.

And don't give up hope if you don't get an upgrade at the check-in desk. At that point most airlines are a bit uncertain about how many passengers will turn up, so they're not sure how many passengers might need to be moved around the cabins. Once check-in has closed and the numbers are set the computer does its work. Hearing your name called at the gate could mean you're going up in the world. And sometimes you get the news even later than that. When you get to the front of the line at the gate and have your boarding pass scanned the green light normally goes off and you're cleared for take-off. If a red light goes off you'll probably have a minor panic attack thinking something's wrong. But if the staff are smiling and they tear up your old boarding pass and print out a new one then it's very good news. You're almost certainly off to a far better seat up front.

Make it all the way on board your plane without an upgrade and I've got to say you're out of luck. The crew working in economy don't have the power to move people up front – not least because they probably don't know where any spare seats might be at the front of the plane. If there is something seriously wrong with your actual seat – and it will probably have to be something that interferes with safety rules – then they'll speak to their boss and you'll get moved somewhere else in the same cabin. If that's full then there's a chance you might go forward. But saying you've got a bad back, that your TV screen doesn't work or that the person beside you smells won't be enough to swing it.

If something trivial is wrong and you're really, really nice to the economy crew then they might get you something extra from the bar, or even a voucher for the in-flight shop by way of compensation. But if something trivial is wrong and you're a real pain about it then you're getting nothing. And if you act like a diva then good luck expecting someone to come when you press the call button. Cabin crew staff remember rude customers and we pass it on to all our colleagues – as I'll explain in a lot more detail further on in the book.

SO WILL WE GET AN UPGRADE IF WE SAY WE'RE ON HONEYMOON?

Are you kidding? It's probably time to put an end to this idea for good. A lot of your cabin crew will be single, divorced, desperately looking for love or desperate to escape a bad romance. We're nice people. But the idea that we'll go all gooey over the sight of love's young dream is madness. If you come over all smug how are we supposed to act? You're all loved up and you're off on an expensive dream honeymoon. Your life is working. We're miserable, we had to get up before dawn and we don't make much more than the minimum wage. So why would we want to make your perfect life even better? Bridget Jones got it right. Smug marrieds are not cool. Honeymoon or not, if you booked seats in the zoo than that's where you're staying. If you're really nice and we secretly fancy one of you then a sneaky bottle of complementary champagne from the trolley is the best you can hope for. Upgrade because it's your honeymoon? Never going to happen. But at least you're in love, right?

WHO IS BOB?

He (or she) can be the most important person on the plane. Bob is the one your cabin crew are looking out for. Bob is their favourite. Bob will have a great flight. And you never know – Bob could be you.

So who exactly is Bob? Bob is the 'Best on Board' – as judged by your bored and sometimes very shallow crew. Getting ready for a safety announcement while standing in front of a packed cabin of several hundred passengers and what are you going to do? You're going to look for a bit of eye-candy, of course. And once you've found it, you'll tell your friends on the crew. 'Check out the guy in 39K – he's fit as anything.' Or: 'Find some reason to walk through Business and take a look at the woman in 12B. She's a total cougar. She's my Bob. You found yours yet?'

And while it sounds shallow it's not always about looks. Some routes are renowned for having the rudest, most demanding and least appealing passengers. In a plane full of entitled, ill-mannered idiots who snap their fingers for attention Bob can be Shrek, just as long as he or she smiles and says please when they ask for a drink.

WHAT DOES: 'DOORS TO AUTOMATIC AND CROSS-CHECK' ACTUALLY MEAN?

It's the announcement that's so routine to cabin crew that we forget lots of passengers have no idea what it means. It's the PA you'll hear when you're on the tarmac at the start of a flight, normally when the plane starts its taxi towards the runway. Sometimes it's a little different. They say something like: 'Doors to Armed and Cross-Check' on some planes and some airlines. And it's basically a crew instruction to make sure that the evacuation slides are ready to be deployed in an emergency.

On most flights every crew member is given an exit door to look after. Someone should be standing by each set of doors at all times when boarding is going on – mainly because you don't want some idiot to grab the lever and try to open one in a moment of madness. If someone did open a door straight after boarding they'd be looking at a very long jump down to the very hard concrete of the runway. On a double decker plane like the Airbus A380 that can be 8 metres or a scary 26 feet down from the upper deck to the ground – and as passengers don't generally bounce you really don't want those doors opening at the wrong time.

The call for doors 'to automatic' or 'armed' is the call to set the escape slides so that they burst out automatically if the door is opened and give passengers a safe, fast ride down that huge gap from plane to tarmac. You don't want the slides to deploy at the gate, because there's not enough room for them to burst out at that point. But you do want them to deploy if something happens as the plane moves around the airport – and for the entire duration of the flight.

So that's why we get the call to 'arm' each door, and put it in the 'automatic' state, when we leave our gate.

The call: 'and cross-check' is the sort of 'two heads are better than one' approach airlines take to safety. It's not enough for one crew-member to set his or her door to automatic. Another crew member has to 'cross-check' to make sure it's been done. So if you look ahead towards your closest emergency doors when the first announcements are made you'll see the drill. One crew member will sort of disappear towards the door on one side, while the other goes to the door on the other side. They'll move or click some lever on each door – arming it. Then they'll cross in the middle of the cabin so they can check each other's work and confirm that both doors are automatic and ready for the flight.

Keep watching and listening and you'll see the final part of the process. You'll hear a bong ring out. That's the signal that the crew phone is ringing. The crew member on the left hand side of the plane will pick up the phone beside that door - but they won't say anything straight away. They'll be on a party line and will wait their turn to tell the plane's senior crew member that their set of doors are safe.

If you could hear the whole conversation you'd hear something like this: 'This is Jennie, doors one automatic and cross-checked. This is Matt, doors two automatic and cross-checked. This is Chantal, doors three automatic and cross-checked' all the way round the plane till there are no more pairs of doors to check. (And while it shouldn't happen as this is all about safety and it's important you might hear one of the oldest jokes in the sky at this point as well. 'This is Alex, doors two automatic and cross-dressed.' It's silly but it helps crew start long flights on a high.)

At the end of a flight the whole process happens in reverse. We need the doors to be armed, or in automatic position throughout the journey so the slides will deploy if the doors are opened in an emergency landing. But as soon as the plane gets back towards the confined space of the gate area we need the slides to be turned off. When the air-bridge is connected to the plane for disembarkation at least one of the plane's front left doors will be opened. And as you really don't want a vast inflatable slide hitting the ground staff in the face at this point you need to make sure that the doors are all in the 'manual' setting – where the slides will only deploy if you manually pull another, quite different lever.

'Doors to manual and cross-check' or 'Doors dis-armed and cross-check' is the command for the crew members to re-set their door accordingly (and the phone check will happen again as well). Doors to Manual is also the signal that the flight is nearly over. It's basically the PA from the boss that cabin crew like more than any other. Once you hear 'Doors to manual' you know it's nearly time to go home.

CAN A MOUSE STOP A PLANE?

Yes it can. And so can a rat. That's what some 300 British Airways passengers found out back in early 2017 when the morning flight from London's Heathrow to San Francisco was cancelled because a mouse had been spotted on board. Everyone had been buckled in and ready to leave when the announcement was made. Passengers were taken off the plane, made to wait in the terminal for four hours while a replacement aircraft was found and only then sent on their way. The reason? Mice and rats have very strong teeth and can gnaw through almost anything – including vital, safety-critical wirings on planes. So it's international aviation law that planes where vermin have been spotted have to be checked out before they're passed as fit to fly. Back in 2017 BA did at least try to defuse the situation with a bit of humour. 'We know almost everyone wants to fly with us to San Francisco but on this occasion there was one very small customer who we had to send back to the gate. Everyone with two legs is now on their way to California and we are sorry for the delay,' the airline said afterwards.

ON THAT NOTE, CAN YOU REALLY HAVE SNAKES ON A PLANE?

You could on the 'so-bad-it's-good' 2006 film with Samuel L Jackson. And in real life cabin crew are starting to see a whole lot of other birds and animals on flights as well. When I started flying the only animals would be guide dogs for blind passengers. We had special training to prepare us for them and everyone was desperate to have one on board so we could take turns to pat and pet it throughout the flight. No-one minded being asked to lay out newspaper on the floor of the loo if the dog needed a place to go, because we loved having four legged friends around.

Nowadays, though, things are getting a bit out of control. People with different disabilities are also bringing 'hearing' or other dogs to help them, which is totally right. But a new trend of having 'emotional support' or 'therapy' animals on board is getting mixed reviews. Tell an airline that you're a nervous flier and that your pet rabbit calms you down and nine times out of ten it looks as if we'll be having a rabbit in the cabin that day. Or a duck. Or a four year-old monkey, as Frontier Airlines staff discovered on an infamous Ohio to Las Vegas flight back in 2016. Or, an 'emotional support peacock', that a passenger tried to take with her from Newark to Los Angeles with United Airlines in 2018 (search that one online to get some great pictures of the bird perched on a luggage trolley in the New York terminal).

Cynics say there are good financial reasons for this new trend. If you want to take a pet dog, cat or other animal on a flight (and as long as there are no quarantine issues between your departure and arrival airports) then you normally need to put them in a proper pet carrier and buy them a ticket, like any other passenger. But get a medical certificate that the pet is a therapy animal and it can often fly for free. Hence the large number of dubious-looking 'medical certificate providers' advertising on the internet.

Money talks in other ways as well. Next time you're online, do an image search for 'Birds on a Plane' and you'll see the scene from January 2017 when a Saudi Prince booked seats for 80 falcons and their handlers in an otherwise perfectly normal economy cabin on his Middle Eastern airline just because, well, just because he was rich and he could.

But while animals in the air can cause a lot of problems I've got to say animals in the airport just make us all smile. The K9 crew at Dallas/Fort Worth and Silicon Valley's San Jose airports whose animals walk around proudly in 'Pet Me' vests to calm nervous fliers have the best jobs in the world. Ditto the PUP team (Pets Un-stressing Passengers) at LAX and the CATS team (Canine Airport Therapy Squad) at Denver airport.

HOW DO THEY GET Wi-Fi ON PLANES?

Well, cabin crew want to know the answer to that one as well – because sometimes it seems hard enough to get decent Wi-Fi into our layover hotels down on the ground. So how do we get it on a plane, flying six miles up, over land and sea, at nearly 1,000km/hour? Friends at Austrian Airlines have given me some of the answers. They say it starts with three satellites orbiting the earth 36,000 km above the equator. Geo-stationary satellites, if you're asking. We then need to get receiving equipment on to our planes – which can take four days of expensive engineering work on the ground. We need a server, WLAN hotspots (me neither) satellite receivers, cabling and an antenna. The antenna doesn't stick up on top of the plane, like a TV aerial. It sort of goes along the top of the plane, at the back, just in front of the tail. Technology then does its thing and Austrian tell me that signal quality depends on things like water vapour such as rain or clouds in the atmosphere – and as these tend to be heaviest down below 10,000 feet that's where signals and on-board wi-fi are weakest. It seems odd, but the higher we go, the further we are from land, the better the wi-fi gets.

WHY DO THEY ALWAYS RUN OUT OF CHICKEN BEFORE THEY GET TO MY ROW?

Catering probably causes more problems on planes than anything else. The food gets loaded on to the plane in masses of big carts before our passengers arrive. We check it's there – well, at the back of the plane we check the carts are there and in the posh galleys at the front of the plane we check the different dishes are all there too. But how much of each menu choice gets brought on board is nothing to do with us.

They tell us that the catering companies use some sort of formula – they work out statistically how many people will pick beef, say, over chicken curry. Then when we've served the first drinks we head down the aisles to see if their calculations have worked. We have little tricks we try of course. If you're bored on a flight listen to see how many words we use to describe each option. 'Hello sir. Would you like the main option, prime American beef with rich gravy, roasted vegetables and new potatoes? Or the chicken?' Guess what? At that moment we see we've got far too many beef dishes so we're trying to get them picked first. Further up the aisle, when a new cart has opened and the tables look to be turned, it can be very different. 'Good afternoon madam. Do you fancy our favourite today, the tasty chicken curry with nan breads and warm rice? Or the beef?'

But pretty much all the time I'll admit that it doesn't work out. We'll have too much of one choice, not enough of the other. And airline bosses are no longer as generous as they were. When I began to fly they brought on extra meals, to try and help balance things out. Not anymore. Today if we have 245 passengers there are precisely 245 meals. We rely on a few passengers being asleep or turning both choices down to try to keep everyone happy. But chances are someone will have to take their second choice option.

Two bits of good news, though, on the food front. If you're in the very back few rows of the plane you might assume you'll be served last and not get any choice of meal. But some crews, on some planes, start serving from the back on some aisles (sometimes just to break up the monotony of the job) so you might just get lucky.

And you know what? If they have run out of the chicken before it gets to you then maybe that's not so bad. Some crew and passengers swear you should never, ever eat chicken on a plane in the first place. They say salmonella and the like can be lurking there – and that jam-packed airline ovens might not cook each dish as well as domestic or restaurant ovens on the ground. They're probably exaggerating. But getting sick on a plane is no fun at all. So I always stick to the pasta.

WHY DO THOSE SUDDEN, SCARY BONGS RING OUT JUST BEFORE WE TAKE-OFF?

These really bother people. When I'm sitting strapped into my jump seat I can see it on lots of faces. People are a bit anxious, a bit nervous, a bit stressed. They've calmed down, they're ready to go after the safety video and all the cabin preparations. Even our nervous flyers are feeling a bit better – and then a series of loud bongs that sound like alarms ring out through the cabin. What the heck is going on?

The good news is that it's nothing serious or worrying. The bongs aren't alarms. They're just a signal from the fight deck to the cabin crew. They say: The long taxi round the airport perimeter is nearly over and we're about to turn on to the runway so this is it. You, as crew, must now be in your seats, seat belts secure, just like all the passengers. This is your last chance to call the captain and stop the plane if anything is wrong. If you don't do it now then we're off. So nervous flyers can relax. The bongs shouldn't be scary – they mean we're on our way and all is well.

WHAT ABOUT THE OTHER BONGS THAT RING OUT DURING A FLIGHT OR WHEN WE LAND?

It's basically the inflight telephone system. The whole crew has to be connected and easy to reach at all times. If you look around next time you walk up and down the plane you'll see lots of telephone handsets. They're near the galleys and near the emergency doors and crew jump seats.

The bongs mean the phone is ringing – and the code for this does vary slightly between planes and airlines. There's generally one

17

code, one set of bongs, if the cabin crew are calling each other, maybe if someone working up front wants to speak to someone working at the back, for example. There's another set of bongs if it's the Flight Deck calling the cabin crew inside the cabin. Generally speaking the person nearest to the phone that's ringing will pick it up. And we get extra help knowing which phone is ringing because different coloured lights will flash in the ceiling above it as well.

Lastly, there are other codes and bongs that ring out if every crew member should pick up the nearest phone for an 'all crew' call that will be like a party-line. These are the everyday and expected group calls that happen when we cross-check the emergency doors, as described earlier. And they're the rare and unexpected group calls that are made when an actual emergency is on the cards. These calls don't happen very often. But cabin crew are trained to stop what they're doing and move fast to answer them when they do.

AT THE START AND END OF SOME FLIGHTS YOU HEAR A WEIRD NOISE LIKE SOMEONE SAWING WOOD, OR A GIANT DOG BARKING IN THE CARGO HOLD. WHAT IS IT?

We don't hear this on every plane. It's normally specific to some of the Airbus models we fly. The noise comes from below the cabin floor and it does worry people – most flights we can see that on passengers' faces. Fortunately it's normal – and it would only be a problem if we didn't hear it. It's part of the complicated hydraulic systems of the plane, the Power Transfer Unit or PTU that gets thrust where it needs to be. The sounds normally kick in when the second engine is turned on as we taxi towards the runway (at the gate and for the start of the taxi we only need one engine fired up). The sounds can also be heard towards the end of the flight as we taxi back to the gate and one of the engines is turned off, but power still needs to be transferred to them both. The noise sometimes sounds like something is straining to happen, rather than happening smoothly. But that's not the case. This is how it's supposed to be. It's nothing to worry about.

WHY DO PLANES HAVE ASHTRAYS ON THE TOILET DOORS WHEN SMOKING HAS BEEN BANNED FOR YEARS?

I didn't understand that myself at first. I thought it was just old planes that had ashtrays from years ago (and some Boeing 747's can be thirty years old, scarily enough). Then when I started to fly on brand new planes I noticed that they had brand new ashtrays. The reason is simple. You can't smoke, anywhere, on any mainstream commercial airline. But we all know that people still try. That's why we have smoke detector alarms in the toilets, and make people well aware of them in advance. And that's why we have ashtrays. We don't want anyone to use them. But if anyone does smoke then the airlines want to give them somewhere relatively safe to put the cigarette out. Stubbing them out in the lavatory cubicle and putting the stub in the toilet rubbish bin – full of highly flammable tissues - would be a potential disaster, not least because smouldering and smoke can be as dangerous as flames and actual fire at 35,000 feet.

On the subject of smoking it is hard to believe that people were allowed to light up on most flights right up until the late 1990s – that's less than 20 years ago. Until 1979 you could still smoke pipes and cigars on most US flights!

Younger passengers struggle to believe that planes used to allow anyone to smoke, anywhere on board. It wasn't till 1971 when United Airlines decided to put any limits on the practice at all. It was the first airline to introduce so-called smoking and non-smoking sections – though these were clearly pretty useless as the smoke from one section obviously drifted straight into the other. As a result, you could be a nervous asthmatic, sitting in supposedly non-smoking Row 14, breathing in the smoke from the person directly behind you – because the smoking area on your flight started in Row 15. Worse still, old-time cabin crew colleagues say lots of smokers didn't want to actually sit in the smoking areas themselves. So they booked non-smoking seats, then got up and created an even bigger, thicker fog of smoke by joining all the others smoking at the back of the plane once the seat belt sand no-smoking signs were turned off.

As I say, it was only a few decades ago that airline bosses realised that it wasn't a great idea to have dozens of people lighting cigarettes while sitting directly above hundreds of litres of highly flammable aviation fuel.

When bans began in the late 1980s, they tended to be based on the length of flights. American airlines started off by making short flights of two hours or less smoke-free. In 1990 anything under six hours had to be smoke-free – and it wasn't until 2000 that every flight banned smoking (though until then pilots were often allowed to smoke on the Flight Deck as their unions said the danger of nicotine withdrawal was higher than the danger of a catastrophic in-flight fire!)

People do, of course, break the rules. And as usual it can be celebrities who get away with it the most. The late Amy Winehouse infamously spent more than half of an hour-long London to Glasgow flight smoking in a toilet where the alarm unaccountably failed to ring, but where her smoke was obvious to everyone within half a dozen rows of the rear of the plane. She was met by her security team in Scotland and whisked away to her hotel without any serious consequences. If the likes of you or me are caught smoking on a plane nowadays we can be met by airport police when the plane lands, taken to court and fined. You can also be arrested and fined if you damage or tamper with the smoke detector in the toilet to try and smoke unnoticed (and despite some people believe, covering the detector with toilet paper isn't enough to stop the alarm going off).

The actual fines and penalties will vary with airlines and you can in theory face different fines if you smoke in your seat (which does happen, believe it or not) or in the toilet (which is obviously far more common). Federal Aviation Administration rules in America allow airlines to fine passengers several thousand dollars – though recent analysis showed that most people only pay a few hundred. It's the same in most other countries where smokers get fined much less than the legal maximums. But don't think that means it's worth a try. The real sanction is banning you from the airline for life – and cancelling the return half of your ticket if you light up on the first leg.

WHY DON'T VEGETARIANS GET UPGRADED?

Angry vegetarians always throw this one at us cabin crew. And I'm not saying they're right to feel hard-done by – I'm sure that sometimes, somewhere, vegetarians must get moved forward to a nice fat seat at the front of a plane. But super-precise catering rules mean anyone with a special meal request is more likely to be left in the zoo, while someone else gets the golden ticket to move up front.

As I've said elsewhere in this book, catering now is a very exact science. We don't get loaded lots of extra meals, just in case people feel peckish. Instead each cabin is loaded with the exact number of meals we expect to need there. The ever-increasing number of special meals (vegan, gluten-free, kosher, diabetic, halal, low salt, low lactose, the list goes on) are all set aside for the specific person, in the specific seat, who has asked for it. So if we've got a veggie meal for Seat 28B then 28B is where we expect to find our veggie. Move that passenger up to somewhere lovely like 1A and we're left with a meal at the back that no-one else might want, while our colleagues up front may have nothing but chicken or beef. So to make life just that little bit easier the veggie probably won't be going to 1A while his or her neighbour in 28A (who eats anything) really could be.

A quick tip. Unless you've got a real medical or religious reason for a special meal then don't ask for one – and take the request off your passenger profile. Most of the time we do have a veggie option, alongside chicken or beef, so you should still be OK. Or bring some snacks from the terminal if you're worried about going hungry mid-Atlantic. The less complicated a person you are the more likely you are to get bumped up.

CAN I GET DOWNGRADED IF I'M SCRUFFY OR RUDE?

It's the opposite of the upgrade question – and it's complicated. First of all, the good news. You won't have to do the walk of shame from First or Business Class back to the zoo just because you're in shorts and flip-flops and forgot to shave or do your hair. Airlines love celebrities and film stars – and cabin crew soon learn that off the set actors can be some of the worst-dressed people on the planet. We won't spoil their day for anything so they'll obviously stay up front. And if cabin crew downgraded everyone who's rude to us then economy would be so full the whole plane would be dangerously unbalanced.

That said, downgrades do happen. And you can be downgraded, by force, right up to the moment the plane doors close, as well all know after seeing the horrific viral video of David Dao being dragged, bleeding, off United flight 3411 from Chicago to Kentucky in April 2017.

As usual it's all down to the over-booking systems airlines use. If they get a chance, every airline sells more tickets than it has seats – on the assumption that a certain number of passengers won't turn up on the day. If the sums work out, and the 'right' number of people are late, get lost in security or find themselves otherwise engaged then all is well. But while the sums do tend to add up in the economy cabins they're a lot harder in Business and First. That's because expensive tickets can be flexible – with lots of them you can change your flight right up to the very last minute. Again if enough people decide to go on a different plane then everyone gets a seat. But if all the rich people up front turn up then it's time for a game of musical chairs. Someone – or sometimes a lot of people – have to turn right rather than left when they board the plane.

Generally speaking it's the computers who decide who gets unlucky. Again, they see who spends the most, who's the most loyal, who needs sucking up to and who can be disappointed. Just like upgrades, other factors can come into play. If they need just one person to move back a cabin and everyone alongside you is part of a pair or a group then you're likely to be moved if you're the sole single. If they need two seats together and you're the only couple booked as a duo then it will be easier for the computer to move you.

Once again, just like upgrades, you're likely to get the bad news at check-in, or at the gate. You should get a lot of lovely apologies. And of course you should get a refund of the difference between the flight you paid for, and the ticket price in the cabin you've been moved to. Compensation should also be offered, including a cash lump sum, lots of extra frequent flier points, possibly a voucher for a free flight or free upgrade in the future.

Best advice from passengers who've told us about this lately is to haggle. Don't accept the first offer you're made. If you made it through check-in and your airline is downgrading premium passengers at the gate then it's desperate. Prey on that desperation. The gate staff should have authority to up their initial offers. Downgrading is horrible. But it can be lucrative, so make the most of it while you can. A night in a hotel and a business class flight the next day – or a free return ticket to be used any other time – can make a downgrade seem a lot better than it first appeared.

IS THERE A MAD MAN ON BOARD?

There is, if his boarding pass shows he's going from Madrid in Spain to Manchester in England. It's all in the three letter airport codes set by IATA, the International Air Transport Association. For these Madrid is MAD and Manchester is MAN.

The codes themselves go back to the early days of flight – airport identifiers used to be based on radio codes from the 1930s and were often just two letters long. When the world ran out of suitable two-letter combinations airports added an extra letter – Los Angeles, for example, randomly decided it would add an X, which is why it's now LAX.

The three letter deal works well for airports who get in there first. Dublin, for example, got DUB, while latecomer Dubai had to go for DXB instead. Most codes are based on the location of the airport, London Heathrow and London Gatwick being easy to understand LHR and LGW, while in Australia Sydney is SYD and Melbourne is MEL.

Other places ignore their location and go for their airport's other name – the most obvious being JFK in New York which had been called IDL for Idlewind before its very rare code change in 1963.

Some places swerve what logic suggests they be called. Malaga in Spain could have been MAL. But Mal, in Spanish, means 'bad'. So it went for AGP – slightly randomly picking the 4th and 5th letters of Malaga and then adding the P at the end for the very simple reason that it was available. Other places don't care, or don't think about the implications. So we can tell people we are going to SIN tonight, if we're flying to Singapore. We can fly to COK, if we're going to Cochine International Airport in India. We can go to POO or to PEE – at Pocos de Caldas airport in Brazil and Perm International Airport in Russia respectively. We can OGL, going to Guyana, while Sioux City airport in Iowa simply SUX. Staff at the brilliant fare-finder website SkyScanner also like Omega Airport in Namibia – OMG – and Derby Field Airport in Nevada where the words in its actual location have given it the code LOL.

Finally, quite literally, I love the fact that 1pm on Friday 13 October 2017 was scheduled as the final time Finnair flew Flight 666 from Copenhagen to Helsinki – so at 1300 on 13th of the month Flight 666 headed to HEL (though to reassure nervous passengers Finnair said that over the 11 years when it had operated the trip, Flight 666 had flown to HEL on 21 different Friday 13ths. All without incident).

WHY DO PLANE TOILETS MAKE THAT HORRIBLE SUCKING SOUND WHEN THEY FLUSH? IF YOU'RE ON THE SEAT WHEN IT FLUSHES DO YOU STICK TO IT?

Everyone hates toilets on planes. And the issue of noise is getting worse. It's one of the unintended consequences of the new generation of super-quiet planes like the double-decker Airbus A380 and Boeing's lovely Dreamliner. The manufacturers were determined to produce less ambient noise so passengers got a more calming flight. They didn't realise that cutting out a lot of the background noise would make the toilet flush sound even louder. In the past you could only hear it if you were sitting within three economy rows of a lavatory. Now the noise can reverberate across almost a dozen rows of a plane – and it drives us all nuts.

The airlines are trying to sort it out. Many have put up signs in the loos, asking people to close the lid before they flush, to cut a bit of the noise. Some have added new mechanisms so the lids close automatically. But the noise is still there – the horrible sucking sound that we all hate. It exists because plane toilets are designed to get the job done – to flush everything away – while using the minimum amount of water.

The first vacuum loo for planes was perfected in 1975 by a man called James Kemper, a worthy descendant of Thomas Crapper who invented the flushing loo on land. Surprisingly it was another seven years, 1982, before Boeing put the first of the new loos on a plane. And they've only really had a few minor tweaks since then.

Part of their success is down to the specialised non-stick surface in the pan. The vacuum suction bit doesn't produce an actual vacuum. You won't get stuck to the seat if you sit on it when you flush – and trust me most bored crew have tried that at one time or another, so we know. It's because the seats are specially designed to have little gaps in them, so a body can't make a complete seal on them and get stuck.

Lastly, you can't fall through a toilet bowl and be sucked out of the plane. It's amazing how many people think this can happens. We constantly meet people who try never to go into a plane toilet for that very reason. Planes are sealed and self-contained units. They can't have holes in the back through which waste or anything else gets ejected.

Which takes me to another, related myth: blue ice. It doesn't exit. People seriously think it is toilet water, expelled from the plane up in the sky where it turns to ice and then crashes to earth causing embarrassment and injury in equal measure. Yes, in the olden days, plane toilet water used to be blue. It was called SkyKem and was because of the chemicals they used back then. But the water was always captured in those big waste tanks mentioned elsewhere.

One last thing, while we're in the toilet. If you do have a problem in there and need help (and bearing in mind how often people can't understand the big, shiny PUSH sign that opens the door on the way in, it's incredible that anyone ever gets out of a loo on their own) then there is a call button inside for emergencies. Press it and a bell and a light will go off in the galley so we'll know you've got a problem. First of all we'll come knocking to ask if things are OK. If not, we know the trick to open locked toilet doors from the outside in an emergency.

WHY CAN'T I GET UP TO COLLECT MY BAG WHEN WE'VE LANDED, TURNED AWAY FROM THE RUN-WAY AND ARE ON WHAT FEELS LIKE AN ENDLESS TAXI TO THE GATE?

Because the taxi from the runway to the gate can be one of the most dangerous points of a flight. Airports are busy places. In peak times they're like supermarket car parks with dozens of big beasts ambling around trying to find a slot to park. We're directed on where to go by air traffic control – but the flight deck have to keep their eyes wide open because things can still go wrong. English is the international language of flight – but in some foreign countries flight deck friends tell me other pilots frequently mix up their lefts, their rights, their stops and their goes – forcing us to slam on the brakes to avoid sudden, expensive and very dangerous crashes.

Then there are hazards that can come from above – including from the actor and pilot Harrison Ford who mis-heard ATC instructions at John Wayne Airport in Orange County, California in early 2017 and landed his private jet on a taxiway, not the runway. A taxiway that was occupied by a crowded American Airlines Boeing 737 that he very nearly hit.

With all that in mind, it really does pay to stay in your seat till you get the all-clear – and we do make it a bit more bearable now we let passengers turn on their mobiles and check emails while we taxi. For those of you who don't think this is enough then there's always one of my favourite spoof announcements: 'Ladies and gentlemen we do need some volunteers to clean the plane toilets after we land today. If you do want to help us out, do just make yourself known to the cabin crew by standing up before the fasten seat belt sign goes off and we'll come by to give you a pair of rubber gloves and some bleach.'

DO PASSENGERS REALLY CHANGE BABIES' NAPPIES ON TRAY TABLES?

Yes they do. And no, those tray tables don't get a proper clean between flights. In an ideal world, parents will take their babies to the toilets where there are normally pull-down baby changing tables. In the real world parents in economy may be trapped in a window seat by a large, sleeping stranger by the aisle. They might be getting the job done while the fasten seat belt sign is on (though please don't do this, parents. The fasten seat belt sign goes on for a reason, to say we're expecting some dangerous bumps so babies should all be taken out of bassinettes and strapped to their parent till the danger has passed). But for whatever reason, we do get babies bouncing around on tray tables all the time. We get food and drink spilled on those tray tables all the time – creating what scientists will say is a very fertile breeding ground for bugs.

As I've said elsewhere in the book, plane cleaners do a tough, horrible job under very difficult conditions. They're often given the minimum possible time to blitz a plane before it heads off again, superficially looking nearly-new for the next set of passengers. Asking around with various ground crews tells me that 65 minutes for a team of 12 to clean and re-stock both decks of an entire jumbo is generous. Most times, on most seats, the tray tables will at least be pulled down for a quick visual inspection and a wipe. A wipe from a cloth that has already wiped, what, 150 other tray tables that day?

So best advice is to take care. Lots of friends take antiseptic wipes in their hand luggage and give the tray tables a quick once over with them when they board. They say it's worth giving the touch screen TV or the handset that controls the inflight entertainment a quick wipe as well. Finally, it's best to forget the 'ten second rule' about food being good to eat if you pick it up off the floor fast. If food hits the tray table on a plane then forget it. One second on that plastic petri dish is probably one second too long.

WHY DOES AIRLINE FOOD ALWAYS TASTE SO TERRIBLE?

You might have a bit of a point there – but none of it is our fault (and it's not because someone was just changing a nappy on your tray table). The truth is that airlines try incredibly hard to make the food and drink as good as possible (even though rumour has it the accountants want economy passengers to be fed and watered for less than a dollar a flight so the catering companies may take a few short-cuts when it comes to sourcing their ingredients). And your cabin crew in particular want happy eaters, not angry passengers.

The problem is that tastes do change once we get to 35,000 feet. Lufthansa and some German academics did a big experiment recently. They had a group of people eat the same food in a mock plane interior on the ground, and then in the same seats when the cabin had been pressurised as if it were at cruising altitude. The conclusion? Eating on a plane is basically like eating with an extremely heavy cold.

The big things are that we lose our ability to detect salty or sweet flavours by about a third. And here's another weird but true flying fact. The BBC tells me that up to 80 per cent of what we all think is taste is in fact smell. And the dryness of cabin air means our noses don't work very well and we lose a lot of our normal sense of smell. It means we think things taste a lot worse than they are – and it explains why super clever chef Heston Blumenthal told British Airways that it might help to distribute nasal sprays to passengers just before meals, though so far this hasn't really taken off. Weirdly, noise affects our sense of taste as well – the constant hum of engine noise makes good food taste bad.

So can anything be done? Airlines are experimenting all the time – with new ovens as well as new ingredients. There's a big thing at the moment about umami – the so-called 'fifth taste' – that perks up a lot of flavours. There's a lot of it in tomatoes, mushrooms and spinach. So expect a lot more of those in your dishes in future – as well as some spicier curries. And if you want to perk up your food, some passengers now bring little sachets of monosodium glutamate to sprinkle on their main meals.

Also expect a lot of on-going arguments about whether cooking and fast-chilling food on the ground and then re-heating it in a plane can ever be a safe or healthy thing to do. Television super-chef Gordon Ramsay sort of let the cat out of the bag about this in 2017 when he gave a typically forthright interview with an online fashion and lifestyle magazine Refinery29. Remember this is the man who has spent ten years on a panel of culinary experts advising Singapore Airlines on its in-flight catering. This is what he said: 'There's no xxxxing way I eat on planes. I worked for airlines for ten years, so I know where the food's been and where it goes and how long it took before it got on board.' He said he always eats in the terminal rather than in the air.

Finally, if you're on a diet it's worth noting that airline food probably won't help you. As we lose our ability to taste sugar at altitude the food firms add extra to our meals to compensate. So while portions may look small they pack a big punch. Oxford University professor Charles Spence says we consume an average of 3,400 calories on a typical long haul flight – that's the same as six Big Macs. And while airlines offer healthy options we don't normally pick them. We often get just one fruit salad loaded on to a typical jumbo – and most flights no-one ever orders it.

WHY CAN'T I GET A DECENT DRINK ON A PLANE?

The same facts come into play as they did with our food. And some wines taste far better than others at 35,000 feet. The taste of tomato juice is sharper up high - which might be why people who hardly ever drink it on the ground always ask for a Bloody Mary in the air. Some wines taste better than others at altitude as well (interestingly most champagnes taste worse up high, though it doesn't stop passengers wanting them). Lots of wines 'thin out' under pressure – including plenty of classic Bordeaux. A fruity South African Malbec is supposed to taste better at altitude than a dry European alternative. And a top tip from a wine expert? If you want to feel good then order your drink as early as you can. Don't wait till after the meal when your nose will have dried out and your taste buds will have taken a big hit. 'Drink little, but drink early' is the word from the wise.

WHY CAN'T I GO TO THE LOO JUST BEFORE WE LAND? I PROMISE TO BE QUICK.

Everyone always promises to be quick but you still can't do it. You can't rush to the loo just before we take-off, either. Again, it's safety. The captain turns on the seat-belt signs before take-off and landing because these are pretty much the most dangerous parts of any flight (statistically speaking the three minutes after take-off and the eight minutes before landing are the most dangerous of all). And there are no seatbelts in the toilets. For landing, the added risk is the one you pose to those around you. If you're moving up and down the aisles when we hit a big air pocket or some serious turbulence then things can get very ugly. You getting thrown up and breaking your arm when you hit the plane ceiling is bad enough. You having your skull crash into that of a fellow passenger you when you come back down will be even worse.

We can walk around as cabin crew when the seat belt signs are first on – but we're instinctively more cautious as we do it. And when you hear the captain say: 'Cabin crew, thank you very much and seats for landing' that's when we're like everyone else. We too have to sit down and buckle up for the first and last sections of every flight.

It's a grey area with what happens if you do go to the loo when the seat belt signs are on in the middle of a flight. Some very tough crew will always get you to sit down and wait till the signs are off. Most will warn you that you're at your own risk, and maybe remind you that you are putting people around you in danger of catastrophic skull crash. But they will let you get to the lavatory as long as you really are fast.

The thing we can't allow is for people to be moving around the cabin during the final, vital phases of take-off or landing. If people don't sit down then the crew need to ring the flight deck and say it's unsafe to continue. A whole lot of people are going to be very, very annoyed if you abort a landing or take-off and make everyone wait for another slot.

Best advice from the crew? It's so simple, but it bears repeating. Go to the loo in the terminal before you board, so you don't have to cross your legs while waiting for what can be a long taxi and take-off. Terminal toilets are always going to be nicer than the smelly box rooms on board, as well. If you don't do that, then you can use the toilets on the plane while passengers are boarding – though not once the Fasten Seat-Belt sign has been put on. During a flight, don't wait till you're desperate till you use the facilities, as that might be when we hit turbulence and the fasten seat belt sign goes on mid-journey. And when it comes to landing, most airlines make announcements 40 minutes before landing and say the loos will be out of bounds in 20 minutes time. Use those 20 minutes to get in line.

And whatever you do, don't be like actor Gerard Depardieu in 2011 when he really should have used the toilets in the terminal in Paris before boarding his City Jet flight to Dublin. 'I need to piss! I need to piss!' he famously cried to a flight attendant who said the toilets were out of bounds as they taxied to the runway. Unable to wait the actor tried to pee in an empty bottle, spilt some on the plane carpet, and was eventually taken off the flight and forced to re-book later in the day.

WHAT ARE THE LONGEST AND SHORTEST FLIGHTS IN THE WORLD?

The longest ones are getting longer. In 2017 Qatar Airways sent a Boeing 777 over ten time zones from Doha to Auckland in New Zealand, landing five minutes ahead of schedule after some sixteen and a half hours in the sky. It had four pilots, 15 other crew and served 1,100 hot drinks, 2,000 cold drinks and 1,036 meals. Also on offer of late is a similar 17.25 hour marathon between Auckland and Dubai on Emirates or a similar length Dallas to Sydney hop with Qantas. United's San Francisco to Singapore flights come in at around 17 hours as well.

In 2018 Qantas got ready for a 14,466km direct flight on the Boeing Dreamliner from London to Perth, taking what sounds like a horrendous 19 hours - though that's still a far cry from the 'kangaroo route' that Qantas introduced from the UK to Australia in 1947. Back then the journey took four days and involved nine stops!

In one way the shortest flight in the world was the first. Orville Wright lasted just 12 seconds back in December 1903. In recent times one of the shortest international flights was the 13 mile, eight minute trip from St Gallen-Altenrhein in Switzerland to Friedrichshafen in Germany that began in 2016 but was cancelled due to lack of demand (and environmental protests) a year later.

In the Middle East, you can go for one of the world's shortest flights on the world's biggest plane – Emirates started flying the A380 double decker jumbo on the 235 mile route between Doha and Dubai (a trip it could do at least 40 times on a single tank of fuel).

Fancy a short flight on a Dreamliner? Ethiopian Airlines has been flying it 17 miles on the 20 minute trip between Kinshasa in the Democratic Republic of Congo to Brazzaville in Congo.

But the prize for the actual shortest – and some say most beautiful – flight in the world goes to the long-established Loganair route from Westray to Papa Westray in Scotland's Orkney Islands. The exact length of the flight depends on the winds and the weather. But it averages just 47 seconds – and while it flies tiny planes the route is so popular with aviation geeks it has had more than a million passengers to date.

On the subject of timing, though, it's worth noting one of the tricks airlines play. Most have dramatically increased the scheduled length of all their flights. In 1996, for example, the typical flight time from London to Edinburgh was a maximum of 75 minutes. More than twenty years later typical flight times are given as 85 minutes - even though planes and technology have got so much better. Why the extra time? The airlines say it's because airports are bigger and more congested and it takes them longer to taxi to and from the runways. But it's really a way to massage the figures. If you say it will take 13 hours to do the 12 hour flight from Paris to LA then you can take half an hour longer than needed and still claim a 100 per cent on time-record in your advertising.

And even here airlines get help. The hugely valuable OTP or On-Time Performance record gives every plane 15 minutes leeway. If you are due to land at 10am, and you land at 10.15 you can still claim to be on time. Oh, and there's one last trick as well. The OTP clock only ticks from the moment the plane wheels go past 3.5 mph on the runway to the moment the parking brake is applied at the gate. So you can be on time at the gate even if the plane doors stay shut because there's no air-bridge or steps and it takes another hour to deplane and get the paying passengers into the terminal.

HOW DO CREW MANAGE TO COOK FANCY FOUR COURSE MEALS FOR FIRST CLASS PASSENGERS WHEN THEY'VE ONLY GOT THOSE TINY GALLEYS TO WORK IN?

With great difficulty, is the obvious answer. Look at the adverts for First Class flights and you'll see how intricate the posh food can be. And what's worse is the fact that while meals in the economy cabins are 'like it or leave it' deals where a pre-done dish is heated up in an oven, First Class allows passengers to pick and choose. If you want your sauce on the side, and you've paid several thousand pounds for a six hour flight, then guess what? Your sauce is going to be on the side. That's why in First Class all the various parts of each dish come in dozens of separate little pots and dishes. A booklet (physical or on an iPad or tablet) for the crew member in charge of cooking then explains how it should all go together.

But we do get some help. With some airlines it's cooking by pictures. In the booklets we do, quite literally, have a series of photographs to show what each dish is supposed to look like, including exactly where on the lovely First Class china plate the carrots, potatoes, chicken or whatever is supposed to sit. (And, trust me, it matters where the carrots go. First Class training is incredibly specific. Put the tiny salt and pepper containers an inch away from where they should be on the First Class passenger's table and you can fail the course and be sent back to fling plastic sandwich packs around in cattle class for the rest of your career).

But life in First can actually be a little easier when you realise that the cattle galley at the back of the plane has to produce enough meal trays for some 300 passengers. On some planes, the galley at the front for First caters for as little as four passengers – some of whom may turn everything down as they've eaten four course meals in the posh airport lounge in the terminal and want to go straight to sleep when they get on board.

With some airlines things are done differently, with actual chefs on board to deal with the fancy meals. These people – who get fancy chefs' hats with the likes of Turkish Airlines - don't have the full safety training and responsibilities of the standard cabin crew. They're there simply to look after the fancy food at the pointy end of the plane. No-one thinks this kind of profligate behaviour will survive the next global recession, so it's likely that most airlines will go back to normal quite soon – and the fancy food in First Class will continue to be cooked by absolute beginners. 'First Class trained? He's barely house-trained,' is how one crew pal described a colleague one day, just before the crewmember was sent to do the cooking at the front of the plane.

SHOULD I PUT MY SHOES ON BEFORE I GO TO THE TOILET ON BOARD?

Oh yes. And put them on before you go to the galley for a coffee or to the back of the plane to do the yoga stretches that are getting so common. Planes might look clean when you first board them at the departure airport. But none of us really looks that closely. And if you looked once you'd never do it again. Let's face facts. Planes may only be on the ground for a couple of hours between every ten or twelve hour flight – and most of the attention in this time goes to the engineering and maintenance crews.

In most cases the cleaners only get about half an hour on board before a jumbo takes off again on yet another flight. So how clean will the floor be, even at best? And how clean will it be after the first few people have been to the toilet? Lots of people struggle to aim on the ground. So how good will their aim be in a metal tube shooting through unexpected air pockets at 500 miles an hour? So remember this. If you feel something wet beneath your feet in a plane loo it's very unlikely to be mineral water. And two top words of cabin crew advice. Wear shoes.

LUGGAGE IS ALWAYS GOING MISSING ON FLIGHTS, RIGHT?

Wrong, actually. The figures show bags go astray far less often than they used to. Bar codes and newer bits of tracking equipment have all helped the situation in the last decade or so. And ground staff say that while plenty of bags do get delayed, very few disappear altogether.

Best advice is to pack carefully and expect the worst. If you've got any important medication then carry it in your hand baggage – don't check it in to the hold. Put a toothbrush and a change of underwear in your hand baggage as well – cabin crew always do.

And label your check-in bag properly. Cheap tags fall off easily – so a better tag is a good investment. I've got three tags attached to different parts of my main bag, just so you know. And a big label inside it as well. In cabin crew training we're told to write our name, home city and email address in big bold letters on a sheet of white A4 paper. We go to a print shop and get it laminated. Then it lies on the top of the clothes in our main bag. That way if all the tags fall off it's the first thing the airport staff will see when they open the bag up to see where to send it.

Better still, most airlines and airports do have an obligation to get delayed bags to their owners. You shouldn't have to return to the airport to collect yours, it should be couriered to you. That's not great if it's a two or three day wait at the start of your holiday. But it can be quite nice at the end, when you can leave the airport with only your hand luggage and know that your dirty washing will be personally delivered to your home at a later date.

WHOSE IS THE ARMREST – ESPECIALLY FOR THE MIDDLE SEAT IN ECONOMY?

Arm-rest wars are a new and increasingly common strand of air rage. They're made worse by the fact that airlines are adding extra seats to planes and reducing all our personal space accordingly – as I've written elsewhere.

So who gets to use the arm-rest? There are no actual rules of course, there are just codes of social behaviour and they're not always logical. If you're in a row of three, for example, the person on the window has the arm rest there and the whole wall to lean into. So they shouldn't lean on to their other arm rest. The person on the aisle, has aisle access and their own arm rest there – so some say that they too shouldn't use the other one. That means the person in the middle seat should get both. Too generous? Or fair play, as no-one ever wants the middle seat. You decide. But just don't fight over it.

And remember it really is possible to share an arm-rest. One elbow can be perched at the back of it, while the other person can have their elbow perched just a bit further forward. It can work. Or, I know, it can end in violence. Good luck.

And whatever happens, it's a bit like reclining your seat during the meal service. If you're in ordinary economy seats then you'll know how irritating this can be for the person behind. The tray table is designed to compensate – so your meal won't tip up or fall off it. But you'll have next to no room to actually eat.

That's why we ask people to return their seats to the upright position for the meals. It's tough, if you never intended to eat and you reclined to try to sleep from the moment the fasten seat belt signs went off. But let's be honest. Worse things happen to people in this world. So please don't go nuclear if you're the person reclining or the person being reclined into. All of this does make people incredibly angry – and emotions are more intense in the air so mild irritation can soon turn to murderous rage if you let it.

As cabin crew we seem to see a daily increase in the conflict over seat reclines. There's so much of it that it's actually covered in training nowadays. We sit in a room, one of us role plays as the aggressive person reclining and we each try to come up with good lines to persuade them to let the person behind them eat their meal. But overall we ask people to consider their neighbours – and to watch their language as on most flights there are likely to be kids around. And to remember that if we have to get the captain out of the cockpit to intervene you can get given a pre-printed warning letter – and you can be banned from flying for us for life.

DO SOME PLANES HAVE PRIVATE ROOMS FOR FIRST CLASS PASSENGERS?

Oh yes – and some! Not every airline or plane has First Class. But when it exists it's fair to say that the cabins are getting bigger and more luxurious all the time. They say that if First Class is full then planes can make a profit even if economy is half empty. And the airlines are going all out to fill those expensive, fat seats at the front. It's at least a decade since flat beds in First Class were enough to entice the super-rich. Now flat beds are seriously old hat. The lucky few want their own suites – or even, as Etihad would have it, their own apartment.

Turn left when you get on board and the key thing you get nowadays is privacy. You certainly don't get rows and rows of seats right next to each other like you do in economy. Instead each big fat seat lies alone. It actually has little walls around it – often with little sliding doors you can close to keep everyone away. It's an individual cabin within the cabin – and there can be as few as just four or six of these in the whole of First Class you're guaranteed the most personal of service.

Back inside your little cabin you'll get a TV screen of at least 23 inches – bigger than lots of people had at home till recently. With Emirates you get your own little mini-bar, just like a hotel room, so you can just reach out for pretty much any drink you want. If you want to lie down on the likes of Singapore Airlines you get a bed that's 38 inches wide and 82 inches long – long enough to be comfortable even if you top six feet tall. With most First Class cabins your chair turns into your big bed – and you get given proper sheets, duvets and pillows by your crew. But with Etihad's The Residence your bed is totally separate to your fat, comfy armchair. With Qantas you can sit, a bit like Austin Powers, on a swivelling chair to address a colleague sitting on an ottoman opposite you. You can also get VR headsets, if the ordinary in-flight entertainment isn't enough.

If all this sounds too good to be true then there is some good news for everyone squashed into economy – because the First Class story does get exaggerated a bit in all the adverts.

Look closely at the photographs and adverts online, and these mini-cabins look like just that – very private self-contained rooms. On Qatar and others you can double them up – producing a double bed – or you can reconfigure the walls so up to four of you can sort of sit facing each other for a private, sky high business meeting with the boss. There are even plans for duplexes on some posh planes where you can go upstairs for bed.

But in reality, safety rules mean passengers can't be entirely out of sight of the crew from start to finish of a flight. So what look like walls and full-height doors in the photos and the adverts don't actually go right to the top of the cabin. Tall cabin crew can look over the top to check up on you, even if your cabin door is closed. And shorter crew can see through special panels in the walls of your private pod as well. That's because we need to know if your seatbelt is fastened during turbulence, for a start. We need to perform basic safety checks throughout the flight. So don't think the people in First Class are entirely in their own worlds.

WHAT ELSE DO THEY GET IN THE FAT SEATS AT THE FRONT OF THE PLANE?

A lot more crew to look after them, for a start. Back in the zoo (sorry, in economy) there can be just 5 cabin crew looking after up to 180 passengers – that's one crew member looking after almost 40 flyers. Up front there can be as few as 8 First Class seats in the posh cabin – and up to three dedicated crew.

On some airlines there are even more staff up front. On Emirates, for example, there can be up to two 'shower attendants' – because there really are showers on board, to the horror of green campaigners who quite rightly point out the madness of using extra fuel to lug gallons of unnecessary water up and down to 35,000 feet every flight. Just go online and check out the first madly controversial advert Jennifer Aniston did for Emirates in 2016 to see how ridiculous it all is. For the record, each First Class passenger on Emirates can have one shower per flight – you book slots of 30 minutes in the two shower rooms, and get exactly five minutes of hot running water. Plus a fruit platter waiting on your seat when you return, all clean and environmentally careless.

And it's not just fruit platters that the crew up front will be handing out. First Class cabins are busy tying up with all sorts of luxury brands. At the back we don't even hand our eye masks or polyester socks any more. Up front you're likely to get goodie bags from the likes of Bulgari, Missoni, Salvatore Ferragamo, Dior or, slightly weirdly, Jaguar or Porsche. And a quick tip – if you do want one of these lovely goodie bags and can't afford a First Class flight they're always available on eBay. Buy one and bring it into economy and your crew will probably notice. We won't assume you're a shy billionaire. Deep down we'll know you're probably one of us and you bought it online. But in the back of our mind we wonder if you're from head office or if you're a mystery shopper sent to the back of the plane to check up on us. So if you ask for an extra Diet Coke then just for once we might remember to bring it to you.

IS IT ME, OR IS IT GETTING EVEN MORE CROWDED IN ECONOMY?

It's not you. And things could be on the point of getting even worse. In the olden days I'm told that big long haul planes with two aisles in economy had two seats on the left hand side of the aisle, three seats in the middle section and then two seats on the other side. That was a grand total of seven seats across. Today a standard configuration is 3-3-3 or nine seats across, though many airlines now make 3-4-3 work so it's ten across in many Boeing and Airbus planes.

In the olden days as well, there was a golden age when people complained that their seats were too big! In 1984 the new British Airways super club seat got bad reviews for being too wide, at 24 inches across. Passengers flopped around in it, they said.

So they're partly to blame for what we find now, when things really are getting worse. Having long-since got rid of its 'too big' seats, BA is now talking of adding an extra seat per row on its new planes, so it may soon be a horrendous eleven seats across in something like an A380.

How do they do it? There are safety rules that mean the aisles can't be made too thin – they're the route to the doors in an emergency after all. So it's the seats that get narrower. In the 1970s the average economy seat was 18 inches across. Now, with the average passenger a lot larger, they are just 16.5 inches across. And there is no legal minimum for them – things could get much worse.

Seat pitches are being cut as well. Airlines aren't just adding extra seats in each row, they're adding extra rows on each plane.

Again, how do they do that? By putting the seats closer behind each other, of course. The distance between you and the seat in front is called the pitch. It's a jealously protected measurement but it's been going down by an inch a decade from the 1970s when it stood at a typical 35 inches. It's now 31 inches or less.

Still, it could be worse. Airlines could hit us twice over by removing toilets to squeeze in extra seats – making it more crowded and having more people standing in line for less loos. But they'd never do that, right? Wrong. Amazingly there's no legal requirement for planes to have toilets at all. And budget carrier Ryanair in the UK has asked Boeing about new layouts for its 737s that will cut out one of the three toilets and allow it to add an extra six seats to the current 189. There have even been rumours that a budget airline has asked engineers if it could be safe to fly people standing up – like on commuter trains and buses. So far it's just been talk and rumours. So far.

WHY DO PLANES FLY AT 35,000 FEET?

It's been worked out as the optimum level for most of today's planes. In theory the higher we all go the better, because the higher we are the thinner the air is and the easier and cheaper it is to power through it. But after a certain point the air gets so thin that there's not enough oxygen for the engines to burn properly.

Good old Concorde used to fly a lot higher – around 50-60,000 feet. But my flight deck friends say it will be a long time until the rest of us get that high again.

CAN A PLANE BE MOVING, EVEN WHEN IT'S STATIONARY?

It's not a trick question – and the answer is that yes it can. I learned all about this from the clever people at FlightDeckFriend.com and it's all about the difference between air speed and ground speed.

Ground speed is sort of the time it takes to get across a set distance on the ground. It's measured in nautical miles and planes often go between 300 and 600 nautical miles per hour (nautical miles and knots are used in aviation for hugely complicated reasons, but they are more accurate over long distances than ground miles or kilometres).

Air speed is something different. It's complicated but it's basically the measure of wind going over the wings. So if we're stationary on the ground, but we've got a headwind of, say, 20 miles per hour blowing front to back over the wing then we've got an air speed of 20 mph. Even though we're not moving an inch.

WHY DO WE HAVE TO WAIT TILL WE'VE TAKEN OFF BEFORE SWITCHING SEATS IN A HALF-EMPTY PLANE?

In a very small plane – the kind with maybe a single seat on each side of the central aisle – it can be about balancing the weight for take-off. Crew sometimes give the same reason to passengers on ordinary planes as well – but it's not true. Pilots tell me that that if every passenger decided to sit on the right hand window seat we'd still thunder down the runway and up into the air OK.

We tell people to stay in their assigned seat till we're in the air and the seat-belt signs are off to make life easier for everyone. Sometimes on the ground you may hear the PA announcement: 'cabin crew, that's boarding complete' which tell us the doors are about to close and everyone who's supposed to be on board is in fact on board. But things can still change. A pair of economy passengers due to sit in 39F and 39G might still be up front, chatting

45

to a friend on the crew, or asking for extra help or information from the cabin manager in the business class galley. If we let someone from 42G move three rows forward for a bit more space then he or she will have to move right back as soon as the latecomers get to the back of the plane. And that can take a bit of doing, especially as the person in 42F may have moved across to get an aisle seat – and so on.

Too much last minute moving around and we can't give the vital 'cabin secure' message to the flight deck saying everyone is sitting down with their seat belts fastened and we're safe to taxi and take-off. It sounds crazy but trust me, a huge amount of time-consuming confusion gets triggered when people switch seats too early (especially when so many passengers can never find their boarding pass in the midst of it, so it can take even longer to get back to their assigned seat). And that confusion can delay us leaving the gate, get us to miss our take-off slot and set us off schedule for the rest of the flight.

Top tip? If there are empty seats near you and you want to get into them get yourself ready, with your shoes on and your bag close at hand under the seat in front. Wait for the 'ping' as the Fasten Seat Belt sign goes off when you get airborne. Then move fast to beat everyone else.

WHAT HAPPENS TO ALL THE RUBBISH?

If you're in economy you'll see that used meal trays go back in the same carts that they were served from in the first place. We then lock them up and the ground crews take them off to be sorted when the flight's over. And on that note, if you look at the carts themselves you'll see that each meal tray fits into a very low, flat slot. So if you pile your various plastic cups, bottles and containers up on the tray for collection we won't be your friend. We have to move it all around so it fits into its post-box size slot – a process that doesn't take long when you do it once, but which soon adds up in a 100 passenger cabin, especially when those passengers are all looking at their watches and waiting to be served tea or coffee.

In the premium cabins the posher meal trays are normally collected by hand and taken back to the galley. We wouldn't want our Business or First class people to see a trolley or a rubbish cart, after all. But once there they too go back into the little slots in their carts. So again, lie your empty glasses and bottles flat on their side and we'll like you a whole lot more.

Most of the vast amount of other rubbish generated on a long-haul, ten, twelve or more hour flight gets compacted. Most galleys have noisy compacters that squash it down so it doesn't totally overwhelm us. Empty glass bottles in the fancy cabins get put in boxes in one of the cupboards, unread newspapers get flung in wardrobes. In the rush to prepare a cabin for landing (when stray rubbish can be trip hazards in an emergency) we just put it pretty much wherever we can find.

WHAT HAPPENS TO HALF EMPTY BOTTLES OF WINE IN BUSINESS AND FIRST CLASS?

Some fancy bottles may get stoppered up and locked away in a cart for use on the return leg of the flight. But all the champagne and a lot of the wine will get flushed down the toilet. If you see the crew sneak into a toilet towards the end of a flight holding a bottle of booze it's not because we need a quick drink. It's to pour it all away.

Old-timers say it didn't used to be this way. They talk of 'crew juice' the lethal mix of alcoholic cocktails they poured into empty mineral water bottles on the plane. The crew juice was then drunk on the crew bus so they could get the party started even before they got to the layover hotel. Today this would break all sorts of rules, not least ones about importing alcohol across borders and being drunk on duty. In theory tough airlines can also see this as stealing. If your airline doesn't want you, and you're caught taking as little as a single passenger snack bar off a plane (let alone a bottle of fizz) then you can get dismissed on the spot.

But don't despair at the thought of the undrunk champagne going down the toilet. It can sometimes be useful along the way. Some crew friends rave about 'champagne hand-wash'. They open a sachet of sugar in their hands, add some champagne and rub away. The sugar and the bubbles mix to form the perfect exfoliator. Rinse your hands with any remaining fizz, followed by a rinse of water to stop them smelling like an alcoholic, and you're promised the world's softest skin.

CHAPTER TWO – In the Unlikely Event.

The most unusual bit of equipment on the plane –Fighting fire – The little hole in the middle of your window - Crisp packets in an emergency – Creaks and cracks – Flickering lights – Mobiles in flight mode – Life jackets – Dimming the lights – Opening the doors – Waiting for the tow truck – Vapour trails – The Bermuda Triangle – Seat belts for dummies – Headlights on planes (and bird strikes) – Handcuffs in the cockpit – The safest seats on the plane – The most dangerous seats on the plane – Coloured lights in the galley – Everything you need to know about turbulence – Lightning strikes – Air marshals – Oxygen masks – Booted out of the emergency exit row – The ABP - Where's all the fuel – How much fuel do we get – Flying on a single engine – Dumping fuel in an emergency - What's GPWS – Window blinds when we land – Seat belts for babies - The brace position - Landing on water – Pulling the red cord - Slides that can be used as rafts – The black box –The Secret Emergency Exit - Landing on a desert island.

WHAT'S THE MOST UNUSUAL PIECE OF CABIN CREW EQUIPMENT ON BOARD?

There's a lot of contenders for this one. But I'd go for the axe. In the past most planes had one on board somewhere (I won't say where for security reasons). It was there so the crew could bash through internal cabin walls to find the source of a fire if there's smouldering coming from a part of the plane that's otherwise impossible to reach. As I'll discuss elsewhere in this book, smoke can be as dangerous as actual flames at 35,000 feet. So if smoke is seeping through the toilet wall, for example, we need to get at it and neutralise it – however much noise we make and however much damage we do. Plenty of planes do still have a hidden axe for emergency crew use. But after 9/11 when security issues got so important a lot of airlines replaced it with a crowbar. This is now the go-to tool for the same fire-fighting tasks. But axe or crowbar we keep their location under wraps.

SO THERE ARE FIRE EXTINGUISHERS ON BOARD?

Of course. There will be several, positioned right across the plane on long-haul flights – and the bigger the capacity of the plane the more extinguishers there will be. There are normally two types, water-based and halon-based, and the one we use will largely depend on the type of fire or incident to be tackled. Water based extinguishers are good for combustible materials such as paper and fabrics. Halon based extinguishers (rarely used on the ground any more but still perfect for aviation) are for wider use. They snuff out fire with gases and can be used for paper and fabric fires as well as for electrical or flammable liquid fires. Crew also have smoke gloves to pull on and smoke hoods to wear so we can get closer to the problem. We also have fire blankets spaced through the cabin to use if required.

Dealing with fire is a big part of cabin crew training. Crew like it, because it means we get to meet lots of local firefighters at our training base. We do role-play exercises, and are assessed on our ability to find and fight fires in mock-up cabin interiors, often in the dark. As part of pre-flight checks we might also be asked the location of different fire extinguishers. 'You're in the aisle at row 39 and a fire is reported in the galley. Where is your nearest halon extinguisher?' Or 'You're in the rear galley preparing the breakfast service. Where are your nearest smoke gloves and hood?' If we get the answers wrong we can be taken off the flight – and possibly grounded till we've been reassessed and re-certified as fit to fly.

To make things safer, there are automatic fire extinguishers in most plane toilets. They aim at the rubbish bins, where flammable paper tissues and towels are likely to be, and where sneaky smokers tend to 'hide' illegally used cigarettes.

Finally, the need to fight fire explains why some airlines' female crews all have their hair pulled up on top of their heads in sort-of old-fashioned buns or scrunchies. This isn't because of fashion. It's definitely not fashion, female crew friends tell me. It's safety. It's so strands of long hair won't get in the way and prevent a safe seal being made if we do need to pull on a fire hood mid-flight.

WHY IS THERE A TINY LITTLE HOLE IN THE GLASS OF EVERY PLANE WINDOW?

It's a bit complicated and it's all about pressure and physics. Planes are triple glazed - there are actually three layers of glass and acrylic panes - and the little hole is in the middle one of the three. The one on the inside of the cabin, the plastic one, is called the scratch pane as it's the one we can touch and smudge while we sit in our seats. The next two are the important ones – they're the strong ones that withstand the big pressure differences between the inside and the outside of the cabin when we reach cruising altitude. They're typical 'belt and braces' things to double protect us all – if one of these second panes breaks the other should be strong enough to keep us safe till the captain gets us down to a safer altitude.

And the hole in the middle pane? It's called a breather hole or bleed valve and it sort of helps balance out or spread the load of that pressure difference, with just enough air going through to do the job as we go up or down. The hole also helps to keep the panes from fogging up due to the huge temperature differences inside and outside the cabin as we fly. Without them we wouldn't get to watch the world go by from 35,000 feet.

So while the hole is always there, and is totally safe, it does still bother people. A few years ago we had to delay our departure and deplane a passenger on a flight from London to Orlando, Florida because he'd spotted the hole and refused to accept it was supposed to be there - even when we brought the Captain out of the cockpit to speak to him and to prove that it wasn't just his window that was affected. The man subsequently refused to fly and he, and his luggage, had to be taken off board before the rest of us could get a new take-off slot and head off more than two hours behind schedule.

HOW CAN A BAG OF CRISPS SAVE EVERYONE'S LIFE IN AN EMERGENCY?

This is another one of my favourite facts from cabin crew training. It's all about being able to breathe in a pressurised environment up at 35,000 feet. The plane engines help pump air into the cabin as we fly, to keep it at a pressure we're comfortable with, and with oxygen at the kind of strength we can use.

If there's a sudden incident or explosion on board, something that carves a big hole in the fuselage, then we suffer what's called a catastrophic or an explosive decompression. Clouds of condensation will appear in the cabin. The temperature will plunge. All the pressurised air in the plane surges out through the hole (sucking out all sorts of thing along with it, including paper, plastic trays and any other debris that's not nailed down). Worst still, humans can't breathe the thin cold air that's replaced the good stuff we've lost.

Fortunately the plane will help save us. The oxygen masks will fall automatically from the panels above our heads, just like they do in the safety videos that no-one watches. We all grab one and we breathe through that till the captain gets the plane down to an altitude where we can take the mask off and breathe the cabin air again. It's dramatic. It's terrifying. But it's pretty clear what's going on at all times.

But planes can become silent killers as well. If there's a tiny crack somewhere in the fuselage then some of the pressurised oxygen we're breathing will leak out. It won't be explosive, like the previous example. No noise, no rush of air, no fogging up or flying debris. In many cases, no-one will even notice what's going on. But as the pressure lightens, and as the air thins, we'll all start to suffer from hypoxia. It's the gradual starvation of oxygen and initial symptoms vary widely and can be easily missed. Some people giggle. Some talk rubbish. Some make inappropriate comments. Some feel very tired and can't focus, concentrate or see very clearly. On the physical side our fingertips and lips can go blue. And if we don't spot the symptoms and do something about it then when hypoxia takes hold everyone on the plane – including the pilot and flight deck colleagues - can lose consciousness very, very fast.

Airplane history talks of ghost planes – where everyone on board is unconscious but the plane carries on flying, on autopilot, till it runs out of fuel and falls from the sky. In 2005 I still remember watching the news at home on the day Helios Airways Flight 522 from Cyprus to Athens crashed after everyone on board lost consciousness – and 121 people were tragically killed.

The good news is that cabin crew are trained to spot the early signs of hypoxia – in passengers and in ourselves. In safety briefings we often discuss it and get questioned about it so it's kept fresh in our minds. As an aside, it's worth pointing out that it was a cabin crew member who worked out what was going on and got into the cockpit with a portable oxygen canister in a desperate but unsuccessful bid to save the tragic Helios Airways flight.

But if the crew do miss what's going on, then that's where something like a packet of crisps can come in.

It's due to that slow, barely noticeable change in air pressure in the cabin. It's got to do with physics and vacuums. The bag of crisps will puff up and out, as the air sealed inside it realises that the pressure outside has become much lower. At some point, when the pressure change reaches a critical level, the packet of crisps will burst. That pop, the big bang that the burst packet will make, can be the wake-up call for the cabin crew. If we hear it and we see what's happened we recognise the danger. We call the flight deck. Oxygen masks can be deployed manually. The plane can do a controlled descent to that lower pressure altitude that allows unaided breathing. That burst crisp packet could have saved everyone's life.

THE WHOLE PLANE SEEMS TO CREAK AS WE THUNDER ALONG THE RUNWAY. IT CREAKS, UP IN THE AIR SOMETIMES AS WELL. IS IT OLD AND CRACKING UP? IS IT DANGEROUS?

The plane might be old - some 747s have been flying longer than most crews have been alive. But they shouldn't be cracking up. That's because planes are actually designed to creak. The whole structure has to be flexible, with a whole lot of give built into the system. The actual cabin where we all are is effectively built on a frame, within the fuselage. It's a bit like a child's toy set. Everything around us – floors, ceilings, toilet walls etc – are screwed into the framework rather than into the actual fuselage. So everything can sometimes creak or shake a little as we face different temperatures, different air pressures and different weather conditions. Pilots actually tell me that we should only worry if things don't have any give or take. Any disturbing sounds or sensations are part of the plan. They're the internal structure of the cabin and they've nothing to do with the solid, vital fuselage that's keeping us all safe.

THE CABIN LIGHTS ALL FLICKERED AS WE LEFT THE GATE. DID THE PILOT PRESS THE WRONG BUTTON? IS THE PLANE IN TROUBLE?

Once again this is perfectly normal – though it is understandably worrying to nervous flyers. If you're really paying attention you'll notice that the air conditioning momentarily cuts out and kicks back in when the lights all flicker. It's just the moment when we switch power sources on the plane. If we're at a gate, as opposed to parking at a remote stand, planes normally hook up to the airport's power supply (and sometimes it's air supply for air conditioning as well). It basically saves us money and keeps us fully ready for the journey ahead. When the plane doors are closed we're disconnected and there's the flicker and air con cut-out before our own engines start to take on the task. Very sensitive, and possibly very nervous flyers, may also feel that the noise in the cabin goes up a notch at this point as well. That will happen when we were using the airport's air and have gone on to our own air con system – it's noisier. But it doesn't mean anything's wrong.

It's the same with the sudden dip in power and momentary change in tone and trajectory you can notice when we're first in the air after take-off. That's normally part of local noise-abatement procedures. In some airports, at some times, we have to alter the pitch of our ascent and the thrust from the engines to make life a bit quieter for those on the ground.

DO I REALLY NEED TO TURN OFF MY PHONE BEFORE TAKE-OFF AND LANDING?

Cabin crew get asked this more than almost anything else, nowadays. In the olden days (that's five or ten years in technology terms) we used to say it was an important safety rule and that phones left on could affect a plane's communications, navigation and flight operation systems. As passengers bring ever more pieces of electronic kit on board - from laptops, e-readers, gaming consoles and tablets – there are fears that so many devices, all seeking to connect to radio towers and wi-fi signals at the same time, may reach a tipping point and really trigger problems on the flight deck.

But so far there's not a lot of evidence that we will be affected. What we do know is that up to half the passengers on some flights can 'forget' to put phones and other kit in flight mode, or to turn them off, before a flight. And as these devices will be sending and receiving signals when they are dormant, and in the overhead locker, as well as when they're used in our hands, it seems that they can't be as dangerous as we originally thought.

Pilots who get angry about this do still say that too many devices can create some interference or echoes on their headsets – they say it's annoying, not safety critical. But most flight deck crew are becoming quite relaxed. Patrick Smith, the pilot and author of the fantastic book *Cockpit Confidential*, says the real risk of electronic devices is that they can turn into 'high speed projectiles' if they slip out of our hands in an in-flight emergency. So that's why they really should be securely stowed during take-off and landing, especially if you are in an emergency exit or bulkhead seat where we don't want any extra obstacles on the ground in a rush to the doors.

And finally, please don't be the self-obsessed idiot (we've all spotted you) who breaks the rules and stays on their device during the safety demo. It's disrespectful to the crew, standing in front of you doing their jobs. And it's dangerous for the passengers near you (especially nervous or new flyers) if you distract them from some information they might subsequently need. So if nothing else, switch off and shut up for the safety information, please.

IF THERE'S AN EMERGENCY, WHY ARE WE TOLD NOT TO INFLATE OUR LIFE JACKETS TILL WE LEAVE THE PLANE? SURELY IT MAKES MORE SENSE TO BE READY – ESPECIALLY IF YOU CAN'T SWIM?

That makes sense on one level. But it's cancelled out by two pieces of hard, scary evidence. In almost any emergency the key thing is to get the passengers out of the plane as fast as possible. The headline target is 90 seconds. A minute and a half. Just think how long it took for everyone to board. Think of all those people clogging up the aisle and refusing to get out of anyone else's way. Getting all these people out of the plane (through the nearest exit which may be behind you, just a reminder) in the dark and amidst some serious panic in less than 90 seconds is never going to be easy. And guess what – we're trained to make it even harder. The next bit of the 90 second rule states that we have to get everyone out in that time even if half the exits are unusable.

So to get this done we need as few obstacle as possible. That's why we tell people to go to their nearest useable exit 'leaving all your hand baggage behind you'. Please remember that one. No lap top is worth more than your life. Especially as carrying that laptop, and the bag it's in, can obstruct your exit and hold back those near you.

Wearing an uninflated life-vest won't affect your move to the exits. But wearing a vest that's inflated and blown out several inches on all sides will. Picture up to 400 passengers on a jam-full Boeing 747, or twice as many passengers on an A380 all bouncing into each other and struggling to get out of small, tight spaces while wearing fully-inflated life jackets and you'll see you can easily double the exit time.

But there's a second, even more important reason to wait till you leave the plane before you pull the red cord and inflate your life vest. If you've landed on water then sooner or later your plane is likely to sink. If the fuselage is badly damaged it can start to fill with water frighteningly fast. In a worst case scenario you may need to swim towards your nearest exit if the plane is going down before you get there. And think, just for a moment, where exit doors are actually positioned on the sides of planes. They're not right at the top – and they certainly won't be at the top if the plane twists as it sinks.

So if you inflate your life jacket inside the cabin you may find yourself floating up to the surface of the water, well above the level where the exit is. As the life jackets are incredibly buoyant, you may not be able to swim down far enough to get through the door to safety. It's horrible, 'hopefully-won't-happen' stuff. You need to think it through to see what I'm talking about. But in cabin crew training we're told horror stories that people who inflate their life jackets inside a plane can drown inside the cabin, while those who followed the instructions were able to swim free.

Finally, the other instruction to clip or tie your life vest securely round your waist is important too. It will keep it on you if you end up in the water. More importantly, it will keep it on you if a fellow passenger panics and grabs it while you're in the water. You won't be able to help them if they've accidentally pulled your life jacket off. So fasten it as tightly as you can before leaving the plane.

WHY DO YOU ALWAYS DIM THE LIGHTS BEFORE LANDING?

To make the cabin crew look better, of course. Or maybe it's for safety reasons. The safety side of it has a couple of strands. The lights get dimmed when we take-off or land in the hours of darkness, first because we want to acclimatise everyone's eyes in case we need to do a fast, emergency evacuation. If you're sitting in a brightly lit cabin and forced to rush out of the plane into pitch darkness then you might take a few seconds to blink and make out everything around you. And those few seconds are seconds we just don't have.

The whole plane has to be evacuated in less than 90 seconds, as I've said before. If you rush out into darkness and have to blink a few times to see things properly you may trip up, fall down, run into something or cause some other obstruction that slows everyone else down as well. So we want everyone ready to see properly from the off. We dim the lights so the outside looks pretty much the same as the inside of the cabin. If your eyes are adjusted and acclimatised then the evacuation should be smoother and safer. It's as simple as that.

On the same theme, lights get dimmed when we take-off or land in darkness to make those emergency lights a bit clearer. It means the floor level ones in the aisles that we talk about in the safety briefing will look brighter when they click on and guide us to an exit in an emergency. The brighter these are – and the brighter the actual exit signs are by the doors – the more likely that we'll all get out on time.

CAN YOU OPEN THE EMERGENCY DOOR WHILE YOU'RE UP IN THE AIR? ISN'T IT DANGEROUS THAT NO-ONE GUARDS THE DOORS?

The good news is that the doors will only open when we're on the ground. It's not due to any complicated locks or guards. It's a bit of engineering and a lot of physics. The engineering bit involves the fact that every plane door effectively opens inwards. It may swing up and out as well. But the first and most important bit is that it opens into the cabin. The physics bit stops that happening. When we're up in the air the atmosphere outside is really thin so everything in the cabin is pushing hard to get out. And I mean hard. At 35,000 feet you get more than 1,000lbs of pressure pushing out on to each square inch of the door. That massive amount of pressure forces the doors firmly into their closed position. Not even the world's strongest passenger could pull them in and make them open at cruising altitude.

And even when we're far lower and the pressure is just 2lb per square inch of door I'm told that's still enough to make them impossible to pull in and open. Though some do still try. I loved reading *Just Biggins*, the autobiography of the wonderful British entertainer and *I'm A Celebrity Get Me Out of Here!* Winner Christopher Biggins – who I once was lucky enough to meet on a flight.

In one chapter he writes about being a celebrity guest on one of the first Virgin Atlantic flights with Richard Branson. It was a party from the start, he remembers. Everyone ate and drank and had so much fun that he, in particular, pretty much forgot where he was. 'I decided after a couple of hours that I'd had too much to drink and that I should be sensible and go home. So I said: "Thank you very much I've had a lovely time," to the cabin crew and tried to open the emergency door to leave.' Fortunately for everyone, Biggins found out that physics applies even when you've had a few too many to drink. The door didn't open and he went back to his seat to sleep his way to New York.

WHY DO WE HAVE TO WAIT TO BE TOWED OUT OF OUR GATE? WHY CAN'T THE PILOT JUST DRIVE THE PLANE TO THE RUNWAY?

Because planes can only drive in one direction – forwards. So when we're at the gate we need to be dragged backwards, into the taxi-way, so we can then fire up the engines and move forward under our own power to the runway and beyond. Turning the engines on at the gate, and hoping reverse thrust will get us back towards the taxiway is a non-starter – because we'd have to rev the engines up so much that we could seriously damage the gate area and harm anyone on the ground working near it.

So we have to rely on tugs. And they are a scarce resource in many airports. Normally the tugs are ready and waiting for us. But when things get busy they can get sent elsewhere. This is when things get really bad and one small delay mushrooms into a far bigger one. If even one passenger gets 'lost' in the terminal and doesn't show up for the flight then security reasons mean we have to remove their luggage from the hold before we leave. Very often we see our tug head off elsewhere as we watch the baggage handlers do this job. And it may be some time till the tug can return, so we miss even more take-off slots.

Fortunately there is a chance things could get better in future. Engineers are working on modifications that can mean planes can move backwards, safely, under their own power. But for now we need those tugs.

WHY DO SOME PLANES LEAVE VAPOUR TRAILS BEHIND THEM IN THE SKY AND SOME NOT?

I love vapour trails. A solid white line on a clear blue desert sky is one of my favourite things in the world. And contrary to a ridiculous urban myth the vapour trails aren't made up of water flushed out of the on-board toilets mid-flight. Nothing that goes into a plane toilet is jettisoned on the journey. It all stays on board, trapped in big, evil-smelling tanks situated just below the passenger cabin.

Vapour trails are something else. TV weather presenter and travel writer Sian Lloyd talked me through all of this on a flight once. She says the vapour trails are officially called contrails, short for condensation trails, because that's effectively what they are. It's like breathing out hot wet air on a cold dry day on land. You can see your breath when you do that. And when a plane's jet engine belches out hot, humid exhaust as it flies this does the same. In the thin, cold, dry air up high the plane's exhaust condenses and forms water droplets and ice crystals that we can see from below.

But that's not all. The actual tips of a plane's wings can cause vapour trails as well. This time it's caused by the vortex that forms as the air rushes around the obstacle that is the wing. In the midst of the vortex, like the eye of the storm, pressure and the dew point fall. Again, water crystals that turn to ice, will appear out of (literally) thin air.

How long any type of vapour trail lasts depends on conditions at 35,000 feet. The cooler, drier and stiller the air the longer they will last (sometimes for nearly a day) – and in some circumstances vapour trails can actually grow thicker after the plane has passed, as the newly formed ice crystals suck more moisture from the air around them and form more white stuff.

The fact that the trails can shift and grow, can come in a variety of patterns and can come out of various points on a plane have puzzled people for years. And they've given rise to a whole lot of conspiracy theories. Some say they're not naturally formed phenomena at all. Some say they are shadowy governments spraying chemicals over the people far below. A quick internet search for 'vapour trail conspiracies' will reveal all.

DOES THE BERMUDA TRIANGLE EXIST?

Talking of conspiracy theories, I couldn't believe it when I was first asked this by a passenger on a transatlantic flight. Then I got used to it. People really do ask about it all the time. The actual area in question is in the north western bit of the Atlantic – near Bermuda, funnily enough. Though its exact location depends on who you ask.

Some draw the boundaries to include about 1.3 million square km of ocean. Others include exactly three times as much.

The main Bermuda Triangle legends all began in the 1950s in Miami, when lots of America was going UFO mad. Throw in a lot of mystery about the Lost City of Atlantis and that's why the initial stories got legs and have been repeated and embellished ever since. Countless ships and planes are said to have disappeared in or over the area. One of the most talked about was one of the first planes to vanish: Flight 19, the US Navy bomber plane on a training mission that disappeared in 1945. It was cited in most of the earliest reports on the black hole of aviation – and still gets lots of coverage today.

In truth the area is part of one of the biggest and busiest shipping lanes in the world – not least with cruise ships – and nothing has gone missing there in recent times. Lots of airlines fly to Bermuda itself – a hugely beautiful island where Michael Douglas and Catherine Zeta-Jones have had a home for years.

But while we don't have to worry about the mid-Atlantic there are parts of the world where we can't fly – though that's more due to human war-mongering rather than alien abductions or other crazy things. Lots of airlines file flight plans that take them around rather than over parts of Ukraine, Iraq, North Korea and Libya. We also can't fly over Mecca and temporary restrictions come and go in places like South Sudan, Afghanistan and even parts of Kenya.

Oh, and the real Bermuda Triangle? It's the one between security and the departure gate in the airport. That's where people are most likely to go missing while we desperately wait to load the plane, close the doors and take off on time.

WHY DO YOU TELL US HOW TO FASTEN AND UNFASTEN A SEA-BELT IN THE SAFETY VIDEO OR DEMONSTRATION? SURELY EVERYONE KNOWS HOW THEY WORK?

'Your seatbelt is fastened, adjusted and unfastened like this. And if you don't know how a seatbelt works then should you really be leaving the country?' is how my friend Jennie Jordan gets one of her characters to ask in her *Tales of the City*-style cabin crew novel *Sky High*.

Seriously, though, there are important reasons for going through the seat-belt demo before each flight. The main reason is because of habit. Most passengers use car seat belts every day, often many times a day. Those same passengers may only use airline seat belts once or twice a year. The belts are different, of course. And as I've said so many times in this book, every second can count in an emergency. Research shows that worrying numbers of people instinctively reach to the side – to the left or right - when they need to unfasten seat belts, because that's what they do in cars. The safety demo is designed to get a subliminal message in there that on a plane the belt buckle is in the middle. It's also designed to subconsciously remind you that you open this belt by pulling the buckle, not by pressing a button.

WHY DO PLANES HAVE HEADLIGHTS?

This does always strike people as a bit strange. Sometimes, at night or on foggy or cloudy days, you can look up to the sky and see planes with their lights picking out the clouds in front of them. What are they looking for? Cyclists? Foxes? Unlit street signs? Obviously none of the above. Once the planes are up the air the headlights aren't really there so the pilots on board can see what's ahead of them. At this point they're there so other planes can see them. And if you look closely at a plane you'll see the headlights are far from the only lights on board. Here's the run-down I got from one of my pilot pals.

The headlights are actually called Landing Lights. They're normally attached under the wings or the fuselage and they're very, very bright. They're used so pilots can see the runway ahead of them on take-off and landing and they tend to be left on for a few minutes before and after each manoeuvre. When we're landing they light up the run way from around 200 feet up.

Coloured positioning lights are also fixed to the end of each wing. Red lights point forwards from the left wing, green ones from the right (it's an airline development of the code from shipping a few hundred years ago when boats first hung red lamps to the left and green lamps to the right). Behind each positioning light are rear-facing white lights, and there can be an extra rear-facing white light on the tail as well. Again, these are primarily there to help other planes know where we are and where we are going. If you see coloured lights ahead you know a plane is coming towards you. If you see white lights you know it's flying away. And while Air Traffic Control should keep track of where every plane is (in the air and on the tarmac) at any given moment, this extra information can be very important when things go awry.

And it isn't just other planes we want to spot us when our lights are on. Headlights or landing lights in particular should get noticed by birds. Bird strike is one of the big hazards of flying. It was what brought down Chesley Sullenberger's Airbus A320 in 2009 – the story of US Airways 1549 that flew into a flock of Canada Geese and became the *Miracle on the Hudson* film with Tom Hanks.

Airports have all sorts of schemes to scare birds away from key air corridors. They blow horns, fly hawks around or do whatever it takes. Putting bright lights on the front of a plane is just one more way to get birds out of the way as we take-off or land. And while bird strike has taken on a very scary significance after the Hudson incident it's worth remembering what a pilot told me when I first began to fly. 'Tell the passengers not to worry,' he said. 'Bird strikes are only really dangerous if you're a bird'.

DO PLANES REALLY CARRY A SET OF HANDCUFFS IN THE COCKPIT?

We do normally have cuffs – though they'll be in the main cabin, not in the cockpit, because that would make them a lot harder to access in a hurry and because we don't want to open the cockpit door when things are kicking off on board.

Crew are all trained in how to use handcuffs. The actual designs vary between airlines and from country to country so they're not always as easy to fit as people think, especially if the person needing to be restrained is uncompliant and thrashing around wildly.

Airline policy and training varies on this as well, but most crews do also have other restraint kits they can use. Basic training involves a lot of fun learning how to tie the legs and arms of a fake 'disruptive passenger' to their airline seat so they can't roam the cabin creating havoc.

Of course this isn't something we want to do unless it's clearly necessary. Tricky issues arise because someone can't be restrained or tied to a chair on landing in case the plane has to be evacuated in an emergency. But kick off mid-flight and all options are open. And as air rage gets ever more common the game is being raised.

In December 2016 the American singer Richard Marx revealed he'd had to help the crew restrain an unruly fellow passenger on a Korean Air flight from Hanoi to Seoul – and it came out that Korean Air crew have been issued with Tasers that they could have used if the situation had escalated even further. In 2017 Russian carrier Pobeda Airlines turned to martial arts and started training staff in judo and samba to deal with unruly customers.

Finally, don't think you're off the hook if you behave badly and survive the cuffs, the restraint kit, the judo and even the Taser. When any serious incident happens mid-flight the Captain will radio ahead to our destination airport. The terminal police force will be first on board to make an arrest and escort you off the plane. So while you might be the first into the terminal building, it's likely to be a long time before you get your luggage and continue with your day.

Behave really badly and your travel plans can be disrupted for some time to come as well. Airlines can and do ban people as passengers. Just because we've taken you to your holiday destination doesn't mean we'll take you back. If you behave badly enough on the way out we'll cancel the return half of your reservation. And guess what? We reserve the right to tell our fellow airlines what we've done. So good luck getting a ticket from them. And have a lovely time on the boat journey home.

WHICH IS THE SAFEST SEAT ON A PLANE?

There's always been a huge amount of debate on this - but I like one pithy comment that says the safest seat in any plane is the one where the passenger is wearing his or her seat belt. Seat belts help whether the potential danger comes from turbulence, an emergency landing or any other incident in the air or down on the ground. If you're on a busy flight and you want to know if any fellow passengers are off duty cabin crew or pilots then look at their seatbelts. If they're fastened then they're crew. We've learned how important this is – and it's one example that's incredibly worth following.

When it comes to emergency landings – on land or water – then then a huge amount of research has taken place to see if some seats are in fact safer than others.

In October 2012 an incredible television documentary - *The Plane Crash* – was screened on Channel Four in the UK and also aired around the world. It featured a team of engineers and experts who deliberately flew a Boeing 727 into a desert in Mexico. The interior was full of crash-test dummies – with plastic, breakable bones inside them, surrounded with cameras and sensors.

The main idea, obviously, was to see what happened to different parts of the plane and the bodies within it at impact. It drew a huge number of conclusions. Some of the solid facts were that the first part of the plane, the first 11 rows, in fact, were blown away in the impact. There was 12G of force up there and the experts say no real people sitting in the first rows could have survived. But the sensors showed that at the back of the plane the force on impact was reduced to 6G and almost eight in ten of the people could have survived the landing.

The study also took a closer look at three crash-test dummies placed in the same row. One had been put in the brace position with its seat-belt fastened, one was sitting normally but with the seat-belt fastened and one was sitting normally and unbuckled. The first dummy suffered the least damage and both of the dummies with their seat belts fastened would have survived the impact if they had been real. The third dummy, not in the brace position and not strapped in, was likely to have died.

Other studies including from Time magazine suggest that middle seats in the rear third of the plane have the lowest fatality rate in accidents, producing a rare occasion when middle seats look like pretty good places to be.

A study in 2007 by Popular Mechanics looked at every plane crash since 1971 and again said seats at the back of most planes were the safest, especially those behind the wing. But in better news for people up front, the research showed that in most crashes there were plenty of survivors from the First Class cabins as well.

The US Government, meanwhile, says that looking at 568 crashes between 1993 and 2000 more than nine out of ten of the 53,487 passengers and crew involved walked away. Even in what it deemed 'the worst' crashes more than half of the people on board survived.

But back to the exact best seats to choose. One final study from the University of Greenwich in London, commissioned by the Civil Aviation Authority says you're best off within six rows of an emergency exit. Interestingly it found there was only a marginal difference in safety between a window and an aisle seat – and it's worth noting that if the aisles are blocked the easiest way for window seat passengers to get to an exit can be to climb over the seat backs in front or behind them.

If you're still worried think about these last few statistics. The overall risk of death in a plane accident is one in 11 million. The overall risk of dying by falling out of bed is one in 2 million. The overall risk of dying in a road accident can be as high as one in 8,000. So the old line is true. If you got out of bed and made it to the airport then the most dangerous part of your day is over. Your flight really is when you can sit back, relax and enjoy yourself.

WHICH IS THE MOST DANGEROUS SEAT ON A PLANE?

It doesn't sound very logical. But the most dangerous seat on a plane can be in the emergency exit row. More specifically it can be the seat at the window, the one right beside the actual over-wing exit. You'd think this would be the safest place to be. You'd think that sitting right next to the exit means you're likely to be the first passenger off the plane in an emergency. But there's a hidden danger in these seats that the crew don't like to talk about.

As a bit of background, the seats I'm talking about are the ones right in the middle of a single aisle plane, where those over-wing emergency exits are. The cabin crew are nowhere near these exits during take-off or landing. We're at the main doors, in the front and rear of the plane. That's why we need responsible passengers sitting in the mid-plane emergency exit rows. We need people to open the doors and to lead the way to safety if it all kicks off.

Some people like these seats because you get a bit more leg-room – there's a slightly wider gap between your seat and the row in front of you (and the row in front doesn't recline) as the gap has to be kept wide in case there's an emergency evacuation. You're not allowed to have anything on your lap, or under the seat in front of you, during take-off or landing as the floor has to be kept clear of trip-hazards. And you will be asked to take a quick look at the diagram on the seat backs and the exit window and agree to follow the instructions if required.

So what's the danger?

It's because of the way the over-wing exit actually works. First of all you pull the cover off the door's handle up at the top. Then, in theory, you grab the handle and pull the top of the door inwards. You twist the whole door around, throw it out of the plane and then jump through the hole to safety. But take a close look next time you sit in, or walk by, one of those exit row seats. Even with the extra leg-room, there's not a lot of space. And tests repeatedly show that when people pull the top of the emergency door inwards they hit themselves on the head with it. The door jerks in fast. There's very little room, and that's when the corner of the door hits your head. It sounds terrible, but accident reports show that the first person out of a plane is often bleeding.

So why don't we tell people this? We don't want to over-complicate things when we explain how the exits work, not least because language barriers can often make it hard to impart even the simplest of instructions. And we don't want to worry people.

But the good news is that you can just about avoid the injury. Even amidst the panic of having to open the door, try to sit as far back in your chair as you can. That way the door will fall towards your chest and your lap, not towards your head.

Finally, as the first to leave the plane, take a quick look around for hazards before you jump out. Flames, rising water and other dangers on one side may mean it's safer to exit from the other side of the aisle.

WHY IS THERE A COLOURED LIGHT FLASHING IN THE CEILING BY THE GALLEY?

It varies between airlines and between planes. But if it's a blue light then it's likely to mean a passenger is being annoying. Or rather that a passenger has pressed the call button.

Call buttons drive us mad – and best advice is to use them sparingly. The buttons we hate most are the ones on old planes that really do still have sort of pictures of a waiter with a drink on a tray on them. Because the buttons are not there to summon up a waiter with a gin and tonic. If you want a drink, get up, walk a maximum of 20 yards to your nearest galley and ask for one.

If you're trapped in your seat by a huge, sleeping stranger between you and the aisle then we might forgive you for using the call button when you're thirsty. But other than that they're really there for emergencies. When they're pressed, as I say, a light goes off in the nearest galley. On newer planes a screen in the galley should tell us which seat number is calling us. And a little red light should go on in the panel above the seat as well to make it easier to identify the offender, I mean the passenger.

Finally, if you press the call button by mistake (easily done if it's on the handset next to one of the buttons that operate the reading lights) then there's normally a 'cancel' button as well. It will be the call button symbol with a line crossed through it. Try that to cancel your call – see if the red light above your head and the coloured light at the galley goes out. Or on some planes just push the red light above your head – that can cancel it as well. Do it and you'll come off our hit list.

HOW DANGEROUS IS TURBULENCE?

The good news is that it's not as bad as it seems. I just read a report saying around 800 million people fly in US airspace every year – and that each year less than 60 of them will be injured by turbulence. Interestingly enough, the report went on to say that of that unlucky group of 60 more than 40 weren't wearing their seat-belts. So that's yet another good reason to follow our advice and leave your belt fastened at all times during a flight.

That's certainly what your pilots will be doing. 'On the flight deck, we wear our seatbelts all the time,' one First Officer friend tells me – which is a pretty good example to follow.

If you want the detail, then pilots say there are four main types of turbulence. The first is connective – which we normally get as we fly through clouds. Then there is clear air turbulence, when we go through the jet streams, long 'corridors' of wind up very high. Third come low level thermals, warm air rising from the ground on hot days. Last of all comes wake turbulence which we feel when we get too close to the wake of other planes.

The connective or cloud based turbulence is the most common. And it's worth pointing out that planes never deliberately fly through storms. In fact we do everything we can to avoid them. Radar can spot clouds (they somehow sense extra water droplets in the air ahead) so they avoid the worst of them.

When we can't avoid the bumps pilots say that we rarely go up or down by more than a few feet at a time, however bad it actually feels in the cabin. They say that however horrible it seems, planes are strong. Winds, storms and air pockets (which don't technically exist, it's just an expression) can't rip off a wing or do anything like that.

The biggest problems with turbulence tend to be motion sickness. Lots of people get sick when we hit lumps and bumps – and medics say that previously immune people can sometimes feel queasy if they're particularly tired or are suffering from any other illness or condition. So best advice is always to check there's an easily accessible sick bag in the seat pocket in front of you. If there's not there might be spares in the next seat. Or crew should be able to find spares from the galley so you've got on, just in case.

If you use it and the fasten seat belt sign is still on then ring your call bell and hand the bag (carefully) to the crew member who's unlucky enough to come along. We'll dispose of it hygienically. The one thing no-one wants is for sick bags to be left, screwed up and probably leaking, in the seat area when you reach your destination.

SO WHAT'S ACTUALLY GOING ON WHEN WE HIT A PATCH OF TURBULENCE?

If we're hit some bad air the captain will flick on the Fasten Seat-Belt signs. So for everyone's safety you should head back from the toilets or the galley and buckle up in your seat.

Then try to relax. It might feel as if the pilot is struggling to control the plane, but that's not how it is. A plane in messy air is not like a boat on a stormy sea.

Unfortunately, when injuries do happen they can be pretty severe. When an Aeroflot Boeing 777 from Moscow to Thailand hit extreme turbulence in early 2017 some 27 of the 313 passengers had serious injuries – all of whom had been standing or not wearing their seatbelts when the storm hit. Many were also injured by objects flying around the cabin – metal coffee pots being a particular danger.

But most of the time, best advice is to try to ignore turbulence and to wait till it passes. It always does. Some say it's comforting to see that the crew carry on as normal when turbulence strikes – though we do have to break off to check that people are strapped in as soon as the fasten seat belt signs go on.

That's why it really is important to follow the slightly confusing message the captain or senior cabin crew member often gives on a PA at the start of a night flight. We tell passengers to keep seat belts visible throughout the flight – and to fasten them over the top of your blanket if you're planning to sleep. That's because the rules say we really do have to see that each and every passenger is buckled up in turbulence. On night flights most crew get given little torches so we can check without putting the cabin lights back up. So if you see us walking around all *CSI* with our pen-lights then that's what we're doing. But the rules say that if we can't see a belt around a sleeping passenger we should wake them up to check.

So do what the announcement suggests. Fasten your seatbelt around the top of anything you're snuggled up under so we can see it and let you doze on through the bumps.

If the turbulence is low level, us crew will carry on with our work once we've checked our passengers are safely buckled in. We'll carry on serving meals, for example, though the rules say we shouldn't offer hot drinks like tea or coffee until the Fasten Seat Belt sign is off again. As I say, nervous fliers do find it reassuring that the work goes on in mild turbulence.

So I probably shouldn't write this, but you might be right to worry if we stop our normal work. When the air is particularly bumpy the captain will make another PA, telling the cabin crew to take their seats as well. That doesn't happen often. But when it does we have to get our trolleys and meal carts out of the aisles fast. We lock as much away as possible in the galleys. Then we sit down and strap up in our own jump seats – and we try to look as if we're not worried at all.

The smoothest seats in a plane tend to be those closer to the front – which is bad news for budget travellers who get motion sickness. And it's another reason not to hang around at the rear galley stretching or chatting to the crew. Some reports show seats just ahead of the wings can offer smoother rides and in extreme turbulence, when things might be thrown around the cabin, some say window or even middle seats are safer than those on the aisles where an untethered trolley could race down towards you. It's probably one of those very rare times when the middle seat has any advantage at all.

CAN A PLANE GET STRUCK BY LIGHTENING WHEN IT FLIES THROUGH A STORM?

Yes – and it happens all the time. Pilots say most planes get hit two or three times a year, though the good news is that we barely even notice it. I'm not a physics expert, but basically when things go well the electricity just passes right through the plane. When it goes badly, there can be damage on the aircraft's fuselage – what the manufactures call the skin - at the lightening's entry and exit points and damage to some electrical systems. But I'm told that even this rarely causes any serious issues for our flight crew.

The thing to remember about electricity is that it needs to get back to earth. Anything it goes through, on its way back to earth, can get damaged. So if you're the tallest thing standing up in the middle of a flat field the lightening will try to go through you to get to the ground – with very dangerous consequences. But once a plane is up in the air the lightening won't get its way. It can't use us to get to the ground because we're not connected to it. So if it randomly hits us it passes through and looks for a better chance elsewhere.

Which means we're in far more danger of damage if we're on the tarmac during a storm – though rubber wheels should again thwart the electricity so it can't go through us and cause us harm.

And for extra reassurance, pilots do everything they can to avoid flying through storms in the first place. Planes don't like big hail storms, for example. Really big hail stones can damage a plane's fuselage and engines so we aim away from them. Weather reports get better all the time, as @SianWeather, the TV weather presenter

Sian Lloyd, tells me. Flight crews get updates throughout their flights – and they'll change flight plans to avoid anything that looks particularly nasty.

IS THERE AN ARMED AIR MARSHAL ON BOARD?

This is one of the questions we're often asked as crew – and which I won't even try to answer as I don't want to give any extra information to the bad people out there. So to those bad people I'll just say this. Yes, there could be an armed guard on your flight. He or she could be sitting right next to you. And one more thing. He or she might not be alone. So don't try anything. You won't win.

WHY DO THE SAFETY VIDEOS AND DEMOS SAY YOU SHOULD PUT YOUR OWN OXYGEN MASK ON BEFORE HELPING ANYONE ELSE? ISN'T IT NATURAL FOR MOST MUMS AND DADS TO LOOK AFTER THEIR KIDS BEFORE THEMSELVES?

It might be natural but it's a very dangerous thing to do. Oxygen masks get released when a plane cabin depressurises – at which point the air in it becomes too thin for us to breath.

In thin, cold air we can gasp as much as we want. We won't get enough oxygen in our lungs to keep us alive. Once the process begins you can pass out very quickly. The stats we're given in training say you can easily lose consciousness within a 18 seconds. They go on to say that the higher we're flying the less time you get. And if you pass out before your kids have got their masks on then their odds of survival are as low as yours.

'It's hard to get your head around it, but you can only help others if you've looked after yourself first,' says my cabin crew pal and *Flying High* and *Sky High* author Jennie Jordan. 'You're no good to anyone if you're unconscious. It might not seem right, but put your mask on immediately so you can buy the time to help those around you.'

On the same note, you should also grab the nearest mask if you're walking around the cabin when they fall from the ceiling. If you're on the way to the loo or you're in the galley then do not – and I repeat do not - waste time trying to get back to your own seat in an emergency. You haven't got time. Chances are you won't make it. If those masks fall down then grab one, immediately, wherever you are and whatever you're doing. That's one of the most important emergency messages in this whole book.

And the good news is that planes are fitted with more masks than there are seats. There are extras on most rows (not least because people with a baby in their lap will need two masks, not one) as well as an extra mask in each toilet. There are also extras by the emergency doors. So even on a packed plane, if you're away from your seat, you should get a spare mask near you.

And as decompression tends to be accompanied by a rapid loss of altitude, and some very big bumps, best advice is to strap up as soon as you get your mask on. If you're away from your seat and there's a spare seat near you then get right into it and buckle up. Cabin crew are trained to do that. We'll mask up, sit down and strap in anywhere in rough skies. We're also trained to 'monkey up the cabin' taking quick breaths from different masks as we go. When we monkey up the cabin we're heading towards where the portable oxygen bottles for the crew are stored. That's the stuff we can use as we move around the cabin to help as the situation unfolds.

Two quick reassurances here. If amidst the panic you think you smell burning it's hopefully not as bad as it seems. The complicated process that gets oxygen to the masks is a chemical thing that can give off a bit of heat and a worrying smell. But it doesn't mean that the plane is on fire.

Secondly, it really is important to remember the bit in the safety video about breathing normally and the fact that the bag doesn't inflate. Recent emergencies have seen people panic, thinking their oxygen supply isn't working because the see-through bag attached to their mask doesn't visibly fill with air. It's not supposed to. Just get the mask on, stay with it and breathe.

Another bit of good news is that you shouldn't be breathing through a mask for too long. The flight deck crew will be trying to bring the plane down to a low enough altitude, fast, so we can breathe normally. This can, in itself, be scary. Going from, say 35,000 or 40,000 feet right down to 10,000 or less can involve sudden and steep descents. People who have sat through it say they panic thinking the plane is out of control or crashing – especially as pilot protocol can be to do a series of steep descents followed by a series of short plateaux, which can feel like a roller-coaster ride.

The final bit of reassurance is that on most planes the oxygen supply from the masks will last for up to twenty minutes. Unless there are big, high mountains in the way, the aim will be to be at that breathable altitude of around 10,000 feet or less a lot faster than that.

CAN YOU BE BOOTED OUT OF THE EMERGENCY EXIT ROW?

Yes you can – and for several reasons. These are obviously important seats and the people in them may have to help out with the doors or other tasks in an emergency. 'With extra leg room comes great responsibility' as some crew like to say. Seriously, depending on the plane layout, you may have to open the over-wing exits on your own if you're in an exit row seat – the crew will be sitting far away at the front and back of the plane on shorter journeys. We have to remind you about this – pointing out the little pictures that show you how to open the door – and it really is worth taking a close look. The process isn't quite as simple or smooth as you might think. And yes, you really do just throw the door right out the hole once it's fully open – but not on to the inflating slide, if there is one.

We can't have any unexpected obstacles in the emergency rows during take-off and landing. That's why you can't have coats, bags, shoes or books on the floor or under the seat in front. And we can't have the emergency rows blocked – which is why the row of seats in front of them don't recline – some say they're the worst seats in the plane as you don't get the extra legroom, but you can't lie back.

So who can get moved on from an emergency exit row? Anyone who decides they don't want the responsibility of opening the door in an emergency. People we don't think can do it – so children, pregnant women, ill or very elderly passengers may be asked to sit elsewhere. In other cases it's a judgement call. We once had a mum in an exit row seat – and her young son, a lad of about five, in the ordinary row ahead of her. If things went wrong, would she focus on the door, or on checking that her little boy behind her was OK? My cabin manager that day decided the latter – so we moved people around.

While I'm on the subject of emergency exits – do please remember those lines from the safety video: take off high heel shoes as they can tear the slides, and don't take anything with you. In a real emergency on a full plane we may need to get 150 people a minute down a single side. That's a very, very steady stream at a very fast pace. If you hesitate at the top of the slide in an emergency we're trained to push you. We'll do it.

Finally, if you want to be a helpful hero in an emergency then you can help at the bottom of the slide, while we push people down it from the top. Pulling people up and pushing them away from the 'landing' area can stop a crush forming there – and can save lives.

WHAT'S AN ABP?

It's an Able Bodied Passenger – someone we think will be best able to help if it all kicks off. If it's a planned emergency landing, with enough time to prepare, we find an ABP to work as back-up at each exit. Off duty crew members are perfect ABPs, and normally come forward in a crisis. Military, police or emergency service staff are likely to be good bets too, though identifying them will be tough in a panic. So the next best ABP is someone who speaks our language, so we can communicate well with them. They're happy to help. They're travelling alone, so they won't be distracted looking after kids or partners. And they're fit and strong enough for the challenge.

Training has us brief our ABPs in the moments before the landing happens. We explain how to know if it's safe to open an exit door, how and when to do it and how to get passengers through it fast. We check they're happy to help if we're somehow incapacitated and unable to do the job ourselves. We also tell them how they can help if we are in charge of our door. When the call to evacuate begins people can push forward towards the doors before the escape slide has been fully deployed. So while we're checking the slide we may need a forceful ABP to block the way and stop people falling through to the ground far below. As described earlier, once the slide is deployed, we often want our ABP to jump through it first and to stay near the bottom, yelling out to get others moving down it and then away from it fast.

WHERE DOES ALL THE FUEL GO?

Take a look out of your window. It surprised me when I learned it. But a lot of the fuel is right there, in the wing. Plane design really is amazing. It's a jigsaw challenge, to fit everything in and find a place for everything we need. Under the cabin floor is the luggage and cargo hold – they need a big space for those big containers that won't fit anywhere else. And as some routes make more money transporting cargo than they do transporting passengers the airlines don't want to waste valuable cargo space with hefty fuel tanks. That pretty much leaves the wings.

In most planes the space is divided up into several tanks, normally including a central tank which is under the cabin in the middle, then there are inner tanks in the wing, closer to the body of the plane, and outer tanks towards the wing tips. The tanks themselves can be big (a Boeing 747 can carry almost 50,000 gallons of fuel while an Airbus A380 can have 50 tonnes of it, after all) and in some you can walk, or at least crawl through them when they're empty.

Having most of the fuel in the wings doesn't just make sense in terms of using redundant space. It's sensible because the wings are where the engines are, which is where the fuel is needed. It also adds weight, and strength, to the wings so they can handle more of the pressure in take-off, flight and landing.

Generally speaking different tanks are tapped at different times in a flight, and the fuel in the outer tanks will be used last as having it there for longer helps balance a plane even more. Some planes have other tanks too, so-called trim tanks in the tail. Fuel gets moved here mid-flight, as having extra weight there moves a plane's centre of gravity and helps make the flight more fuel efficient.

AND HOW MUCH FUEL DO PLANES CARRY?

A huge amount, as I said before. Up to 50 tonnes of it, on an Airbus A380 going on a very long journey. But the exact amount will depend on plenty of things. Flight deck crews do a lot of calculations before every flight – as cabin crew I watch them to it, sometimes, in the operations rooms at our home airports. They're checking and working out a load of things, including how much fuel we'll need.

The total fill will depend on the conditions we're expecting on the trip – the head or tail winds, the general weather and so on. But don't worry about us running out. We don't just carry enough to get us from A to B. The actual calculation is to load enough fuel to get us from our departure to destination airport in that day's specific weather conditions. We then top it up with enough to get us to do an aborted landing at that destination airport, to fly on to the next nearest airport, to then circle around that next nearest airport for 30 minutes before finally landing there – and to still have 10 per cent of our original fuel load in our tanks.

CAN MY PLANE FLY WITH JUST ONE ENGINE?

Yes it can – and if it's got more than one engine to start with it can certainly fly with at least one engine down. My flight deck friends tell me they're trained – and constantly re-trained – to cope in all sorts of emergency situation including a total loss of engine power.

And while we don't want this to happen, planes can glide, even if all the engines fail. We can go twenty or thirty minutes like that from normal cruising altitude, I'm told. And to be honest, we normally glide into a landing anyway, my pilot pals say we're often at idle or minimum thrust as we come towards the runway. So don't worry too much about engine failure. We need the engines to get us up into the air – when a Boeing 747 needs to get us moving down the runway at around 180 mph, for example. But we don't need them quite as much to get us back down.

In the olden days this wasn't really recognised – there was just a general feeling that the more engines the better. That's why four engine Boeing 747s were the workhorse long-haul planes. Now planes with two engines are certified to go on most of the long routes that used to be reserved for planes with four.

It's all about something called at ETOPS rating that shows how long (not how far) a plane can fly on one engine. A Boeing 777 can have an ETOPS of 330, so it can fly for up to 330 minutes in this worst case scenario. And ETOPS, by the way, stands for Extended Twin-engine Operations – not, as pilots used to say, 'Engines Turn Or Passengers Swim'.

The old ETOPS-style idea was that twin engine planes couldn't ever go more than 60 minutes from the nearest landing strip. That pretty much ruled out long flights over big oceans. Today's regimes of extra maintenance, tougher checks, better fire suppression and emergency systems means planes should be able to go far further in a crisis.

And if you're still feeling a bit nervous here's one last reassuring fact. Most of my pilot friends say that despite all the training, they've never experienced an engine failure in real life. Better still, the safety statistics show most pilots are likely to go their entire careers without one.

DO PLANES REALLY 'DUMP' FUEL BEFORE EMERGENCY LANDINGS?

Sometimes they do – though only in an emergency as there will be real financial and environmental costs. Planes have two key weights to worry about: their maximum safe take-off weight and their maximum safe landing weight. The two are very different, as at the start of a long haul flight a plane will be laden with fuel and at the end it should be running towards empty (a Boeing 747 burns around a gallon of fuel a second during a flight).

Land too heavy and a plane can suffer severe structural damage – or even break apart. So if an engineering, medical or other emergency forces a long haul plane to land shortly after take-off it can only do so by ditching vast amounts of fuel into the atmosphere before it heads down. The good news for people on the ground is that kerosene should just dissipate into the atmosphere at altitude rather than raining down to ground in a very dangerous, flammable cascade.

But it won't be a quick process. Pilots have to go through quite a complicated set of procedures to start offloading fuel, as you don't want it happening by mistake. It can then take over an hour to jettison enough to bring the plane down to a safe landing weight – during which time the plane will have to circle the airport where it's hoping to land.

To make matters a bit more complicated, not every plane is designed to ditch fuel. Generally speaking the likes of the Boeing 737 and Airbus A320 don't let it happen so if these planes need to land early they may have to fly round in circles for several hours to burn fuel naturally and get to that safe landing weight.

If there's a clear and present danger and the pilots decide they can't wait this long then a plane can land overweight and risk the structural problems that can ensue. In these very rare cases the skill of the pilot, and the support of ground staff, will come into their own. Foam producing fire engines and support vehicles will be right there ready to run alongside the plane as it reaches the runway in case the undercarriage snaps. And the Captain will do everything he or she can to ensure it doesn't.

I HEARD A PILOT MENTION 'GPWS' – IS THAT A PLANE'S GPS?

No. It's something quite different. It's the Ground Proximity Warning System. It's the recorded female voice you might have heard in airplane disaster films. The one that says: 'Pull up' and warns the flight deck crew that they are too close to the ground at the wrong time.

And in terms of getting from A to B, pilots use a variety of means, including good old fashioned mapping of where known landmarks are on the ground – normally rivers, towns or coastlines. Radio transmitters and other things can help as well. But funnily enough it is good old GPS that helps pilots because it works up high just as well as on the ground.

Finally, some other flying jargon. Some crew refer to SLF, Self-Loading Freight, which are passengers. There's SEP, Safety and Emergency Procedures (not Somebody Else's Problem) and there are UM's (Unaccompanied Minors, and not Unaccompanied Monsters as my lovely pal and author of ConfessionsOfATrolleyDolly.com says). And you really don't want to know what CSD has been turned into. (It's officially a Cabin Service

Director, though to some crew it will always be a Blah who Stands at the Doors).

WHY DO CABIN CREW ASK US TO OPEN THE WINDOW BLINDS FOR LANDING?

Two reasons, both to do with safety. The first is similar to the one about dimming the cabin lights when we take-off or land in the hours of darkness. We want everyone's eyes to be adjusted and acclimatised to the light level outside, in case we all need to get off the plane in a hurry.

The second is so the cabin crew, and passengers, can see potential hazards outside if that emergency evacuation is needed. If there's a fire on the right hand wing, we won't want to use the over-wing exit on that side of the plane and we'll guide everyone to the other side or to the exits at the front or rear of the plane. But we may only know about the fire if the window blinds are up.

If we land on water then things can be very disorienting. One side of the plane may be far lower in the water than the other, and that may not be immediately obvious unless we can see outside straight away. The pressure of that water may make it harder, or impossible, to open the doors on one side of the plane, so the evacuation can go smoother if everyone heads to alternative exits on the other side.

Which reminds me – that's why the safety briefings always talk about: 'Your nearest useable exit' with the emphasis on the word 'useable'. Not every exit will be available to you in an emergency. So cabin crew advice is always to make a mental note of at least two different nearby doors. Some passengers say they feel a little foolish if they actually turn around in the safety briefing to look at an exit when those words come up: 'Bearing in mind that your nearest useable exit may be behind you'. Don't feel foolish. I always look behind me, when I'm flying as a passenger, even though I know plane layouts like the back of my hand.

It also pays to count the number of rows to you nearest exists as well. That's because if something goes wrong you want to be able to act on instinct. If the lights have one out and the plane's undercarriage has snapped off things will be incredibly disorientating. The whole cabin may be full of thick, dark smoke, to make things even more difficult. So you want to already know where your first, second and even third choice exits are.

HOW DO BABY SEAT-BELTS WORK? AND WHY CAN'T I KEEP MY BABY IN A BASINETTE FOR THE WHOLE FLIGHT?

Baby belts are the same as the ones we offer larger customers who can't get an ordinary belt around their waist – but they work in a slightly different way. Crew are supposed to keep an eye out for babies as we check the cabin before take-off and to hand out belts as required. We're also supposed to check that people know how to use them – and to explain if not. If you don't get one or don't get how they work then ask – having your baby properly strapped in is such a vital safety task. Do not believe that you'll be able to hold on to your child in the confusion of a roller-coaster ride emergency descent or decompression (when you may need both hands to grab oxygen masks and fend off any coffee pots and lap tops that are flying though the suddenly freezing cabin air).

With a baby belt, your belt should click around your own waist as normal. But before you fasten it, thread one side through the loop on the extension. Then fasten this extension round your baby. Do not just click the extension on to one end of your belt to produce one long belt that you fasten around the two of you. It sounds complicated, written down, but it makes sense when you're there. And again, crew know how important this is, so we won't mind if we have to do extra explanations.

During the cruise many planes have pull-down shelves at the front of cabin sections where we can put baby cots or basinets. Again, we're trained in setting these up and fastening them down to the shelf so we'll get that done for you as early in the flight as possible. And this is the annoying thing. If the flight deck crew think we've got some bumpy weather ahead and they turn on the Fasten Seat Belt signs then your baby has to come out of the basinet and get strapped back to your lap. Even if they've just nodded off, for the first time in the flight.

Why? It's a horrible thing to write. But just think what would happen to your baby if the plane suddenly dipped in what we call an air pocket. While the plane and everything fixed to the fuselage (including every strapped in passenger) goes down your baby will shoot up. They really could hit the cabin roof. So please, follow the crew's instructions. When the seat belt sign is on, babies have to be out of their cots and strapped into our laps.

WHY DO YOU PUT YOUR HANDS ONE ON TOP OF THE OTHER IN THE BRACE POSITION?

Different airlines recommend different brace positions. Different seats in different planes lend themselves to different positions as well – if you're sitting facing rearwards in a British Airways business class seat, for example, then your brace position is different to that of your forward-facing neighbour. If you're in a tight economy cabin it's easy to follow the instruction on many American airlines to put your hands on top of the seat back in front of you. If you're in a front row seat or a wider spaced cabin you might be told to take a slightly different pose. So do please look at the little drawing on the laminated safety card. It will only take a few moments but it can save your life.

The key thing about the brace position is to protect your body and bones from impact – the force of sudden stops can be extreme – and to protect you from any debris that may fly across the cabin at the same time. In a genuine emergency everything from laptops, coffee pots and even glass wine bottles can fly around doing enormous damage.

So how do we position our actual hands? If you explain the brace position to people and ask them to try it, most times people interlock their fingers when they put their hands over their heads. But impact studies have shown that this is dangerous. The force of impact can send your hands crashing and cracking forward and together. It can break interlocked fingers. And if your fingers are broken you might not be able to open your seat belt. Imagine trying to open that belt right now, if you were panicking, in pain, and couldn't use your fingers. That's why we put one hand firmly on top of the other instead. The studies show that protects our fingers and can save lives.

On that same, sobering note, it's worth noting the foot position we're told to adopt in an emergency landing as well. Look at the crew on a normal landing. They should be sitting with both feet flat and firmly on the ground, feet and knees close together and toes slightly behind the knees. Safety analysis shows that if your feet are in this position in an emergency landing there's less chance that you'll break your ankles, shins or your legs in the sudden stop of impact. And if you want to get out of that plane in under 90 seconds your ankles, shins and legs are three things you're going to need.

AND CAN PLANES REALLY LAND ON WATER AND SURVIVE?

Of course they can – as good old captain Chelsey 'Sully' Sullenberger showed in the real-life emergency landing that turned into the book and film of *The Miracle on the Hudson*. This was when a bird-strike took out his engines and forced him to land an Airbus A320 with 155 passengers and crew on to the river alongside Manhattan.

Pilots are taught that an ideal landing site needs five key features. It should be straight, flat, long, strong and well lit. The long bit means, ideally, at least a mile. The strong bit is important because planes are incredibly heavy – an Airbus A380 can weigh up to 400 tons – so it needs something structurally sound to land on.

Water can be straight, flat and long, and three out of five ain't bad. But it's not going to be strong and it's unlikely to be well-lit at night. But while a water landing won't be easy it's not automatically game over for everyone on board and the longer a crew have to prepare the better our chances will be. Landing on water is going to be terrifying. But cabin and flight deck crew do a lot of training for this. And we wouldn't bother if there was no point. We do it because we want everyone to survive.

WHAT'S THE RED CORD THEY ASK US TO PULL WHEN OPENING THE EMERGENCY DOORS?

This shouldn't really be something our passengers should have to worry about – though it does get a mention in most safety videos and it is worth knowing about, just in case.

It's about the evacuation slides. These should unfurl and inflate automatically the moment a plane door is opened in an emergency – and if you go online you can see plenty of videos of this happening. The red cord, which you'll see somewhere around the edge of the doorway when it's open, is a 'just in case' thing that's there if there's any malfunction. Pull it, and if the slide hasn't already burst out of the fuselage and inflated, then it should do so now.

On the same part of the plane, if you do look around an emergency door, you'll see a 'grab handle' built into the fuselage. It's there for the cabin crew in the event of an emergency. If we're doing an evacuation we need to get everyone out before we leave ourselves – it's like the captain of a ship being the last to get into the lifeboats. We're trained to do a sweep of the cabin – and to look into the toilets – before leaving to make sure everyone is safe. It means we need to be on board right to the end – and the grab handle is there for us to hold on to, as the surge of passengers rushes to the emergency slide. Without it we can get pushed out of the plane before our jobs are done.

SO AFTER A WATER LANDING DO THE ESCAPE SLIDES REALLY 'DETACH TO FORM LIFE RAFTS' IN AN EMERGENCY?

Most of them do – the laminated safety card near your seat should show which ones do, and which exits may instead take you out on to the wing.

Escape slides start to inflate the moment they are activated when the door opens in an emergency. It's an explosive event and the slides should unpack themselves, form their shape and be fully solid within an absolute maximum of 10 seconds.

As long as the slides don't take passengers towards any obvious hazards then the crew will get every nearby passenger down them fast – remembering the safety demand that an entire plane can be emptied, even in darkness, within just 90 seconds.

With that job done, if we're in water and there's a danger that the fuselage will sink then we don't want to be clinging to a slide that will go down with it. Crew are trained to detach them – and there should be a member of crew at each exit and therefore on each raft. It's not an easy manoeuvre, to be honest, and it varies a bit between plane types. You basically lift up a flap and pull a 'detach handle'. It may not sound logical, but at this point you will still be attached, by a rope, though this automatically breaks loose if the fuselage does sink. And for extra piece of mind, a knife will be wrapped in the detach area so we can cut the line if required.

As I say, there should be a crew member on each raft for all of this. But there will be big, bright written instructions, in English, by the base of the door where the slide/raft is attached. Follow the two or three steps and the slide is detached and floating free.

For further peace of mind, life rafts also have canopies built in to them, to protect passengers from sun or weather. And planes contain 'survival packs' including flares that crew are again trained to use if help can't seem to spot us.

It's also worth noting that cabin crew training involves long stretches in a local pool where you prove you can swim and carry out a load of other important manoeuvres for occasions such as these. They are tough days – and if we fail the tests we can't fly. But they're important because in real life it is going to be so much worse. Climbing up over the high sides and into a life raft is hard enough in a pool – that's one of the tests we have to pass. But no-one wants to think about having to do it in the dark in a stormy ocean. So if you're unlucky enough to ever be in an evacuation over water get into the raft fast and stay there. Form human chains. Cling to each other. Don't let your fellow passengers go. Your lives can depend on it.

That said, if you do get separated from other people and you're not on the life raft then remember that bit in the safety video about your life jacket being equipped with a light and a whistle? This is when you might need them.

WHERE IS THE BLACK BOX?

There's lots to say on this – starting with the fact that there can actually be two black boxes on a plane. And that neither of them are black.

They're the things accident investigators are desperate to find after a plane crash or other incident. One is the FDR or Flight Deck Recorder, the other the CVR or Cockpit Voice Recorder. They can be separate boxes, or they can be combined into one unit. In both cases they'll actually be painted bright orange, to make them easier to find. They'll also be encased in a super-strong stainless steel or titanium shell designed to survive temperatures of up to 1,000 degrees Celsius and massive crash impacts. And while they record events in the cockpit, they're actually built into the tail of the plane – as that's just a little bit more protected in the event of a head-on crash landing.

The FDR collects vast amounts of data every second of a flight. It records details of every flight critical, and other, bit of information. From air speed, acceleration, altitude, flap settings, outside temperature, cabin temperature, cabin pressure – the list goes on and on. Every switch that the flight deck crew flick is recorded. Every action they take can be analysed after the event – and there should be enough room on the FDR to record the whole of even the longest flight, so there will be a record of something that occurs early, but has repercussions later.

The CVR gets its information from a set of microphones in the flight deck. Some are in the headsets worn by the flight crew. Others are in the fuselage, so they will record any extra or unusual sounds, or conversations by others in the cockpit. It means any instructions from air traffic control, any responses or comments from the flight deck crew, and any other conversations can be analysed by crash or incident investigators. One drawback to the current CVR system is that investigators can't relive the entire flight. The recorders tend to use 30 minute loops – they record half an hour of sound, then return to the start, wiping the old record as they go.

If the worst happens, black boxes are designed to be found. They have water-activated Underwater Location Beacons or ULBs, which emit a ping every minute for 30 days to help them get found if a plane crashes at sea. The boxes are also designed to survive. The black box for Air France flight 447 that crashed off the coast of Brazil in 2009 wasn't found for nearly two years. But its data could still be read, despite the box surviving the impact and lying 13,000 feet down in salty corrosive water since the crash.

In the future, there are calls for extra information to be collected – including video cameras in cockpits. There is talk of having a second, self-ejecting black box on a plane, to make it easier to find the vital information soon when a crisis hits in a remote location. And, of course, there's the possibility to live stream all the data direct to the ground to remove the need for a black box altogether.

IS IT TRUE THERE'S A SECRET EMERGENCY EXIT FOR A REAL EMERGENCY?

There can be. But if you need to use it then things have gone very wrong with your day. The best time to see it is if you board a plane using steps from the tarmac. Look along the fuselage. Somewhere you may see some small red marks painted round a window. Look closer and it should say: CUT HERE IN EMERGENCY. It's a marker for fire crews, to tell them that the fuselage is deliberately weaker at this point. So this is where they get the metal cutting torches going to prize through the plane's hull to open it up if there is absolutely on other way out.

WHAT IF WE CRASH LAND ON A DESERT ISLAND? OR THE MIDDLE OF AN ACTUAL DESERT? OR HIGH UP IN THE MOUNTAINS?

Hopefully your airline has got this at least partially covered. Most of the time, of course, emergency landings take place at airports. When something goes wrong the crew in the cockpit normally has time to find and radio ahead to the nearest airport, even if it's one they've never used before. The airport then has time to get a fire and medical crew ready so they can prepare for any eventuality.

If a plane actually comes down far from a landing strip – and far from any emergency service vehicles and staff – then rescue should be scrambled to arrive fast. But in the meantime most big commercial airlines have survival kits on board to help us through the time we might be on our own. Cabin crew are trained to take these out of the plane just before leaving themselves – and after checking that every passenger is safely off (we're trained to check the toilets and do a sweep through the cabin first as well).

The survival kits are hefty, sealed units, often stored up in the cabin ceiling. They contain a variety of emergency kit – including sun and storm canopies that can offer weather protection at sea or on land. There's extra medical kit (though crew are also told to grab the other medical kits before they evacuate as well) and even slightly unusual items like lip salves (because the survival experts airlines get advice from say lips can take a surprisingly harsh beating in extreme locations). There should be torches and flashlights. There should be day and night flares as well as other signalling devices including beacons and glow sticks. Raft repair kits and water purification tablets should be there as well.

Contrary to some reports there's no extra emergency food rations – though there can be glucose or sucrose for a real crisis. Obviously none of this should ever need to be used – no-one I have ever flown with has ever had to do so. But if you're a nervous flyer it's probably good to know it's there.

CHAPTER THREE – Fit to Fly.

Delivering a baby – Is there a doctor on board - Sunburn on a plane – Flying with a cold – Feeling bloated (and 'crop dusting') – Sleeping pills – Popping ears – Coffee and tea – Afraid of flying - Drinking on board – Drinking in the terminal – E-cigarettes on board – Flying after surgery – Flying with broken bones – Flying after scuba – Dead bodies – Flying in contact lenses – Too fat to fly – Deep Vein Thrombosis – Needing extra oxygen on a flight - How to beat jet lag.

DO CABIN CREWS REALLY KNOW HOW TO DELIVER A BABY ON BOARD?

You bet. Medical and first aid training is hugely important for cabin crew round the world. It's taught intensively in initial training and it's fully refreshed at least once a year. A lot of it is general, basic stuff, dealing with minor bumps, burns and scrapes. But crew are trained to be ready for a lot more as well – from panic attacks to heart attacks and, yes, to the unexpected mid-flight arrival of a brand new little passenger.

Planes should all have sealed, up-to-date first aid boxes for a variety of different scenarios. Each galley areas should contain a basic box with sticking plasters, suture strips, eye drops and pads, headache, motion sickness and diarrhoea pills and the like. There's normally paperwork to be done whenever the seals are broken and if you need a headache pill for example, you'll probably have to sign a bit of paper saying why. The note will include your seat number, so you can't later accuse the crew of giving you something inappropriate.

Elsewhere in the plane, normally up front, there should also be a more hard-core box with a lot of extra kit and different meds. It will include bio-hazard bags, a GTN spray for chest pain/angina attacks, glucose gels for diabetics, plus a variety of kit and cures for people in all sorts of other trouble.

If something really serious happens then planes should also have charged-up defibrillators for heart attack patients – and all crew are trained and regularly re-trained in how to use them.

And, yes, there's also a sterile birthing kit for a premature birth, containing forceps, umbilical clamps and so on. The good news is that while crews get specific training for it, babies aren't actually born on flights all that often – not least because 'fit to fly' rules. These mean you really shouldn't show up for boarding when you know you'd be better off at a maternity ward. Rules vary between airlines and around the world, but generally speaking a mum-to-be can fly as late as 36 or 37 weeks into a pregnancy (less if you're expecting twins or more) – but after 28 weeks you do normally need to have visited your doctor first. Most airlines will want an official doctors' letter confirming the date your baby is due. And yes, expect visual checks and questions at check-in, at the gate, and on the plane itself. Expectant parents have a host of different reasons for trying to hide how far they are into a pregnancy – or even that they are pregnant at all. And as we don't want to break out that birthing kit when we've got gin and tonics to serve we'd rather be safe than sorry and leave you on the ground if you've not followed the rules.

That said, babies are babies – and they can sometimes surprise everyone by arriving well ahead of schedule. And when that does happen the stories can have happy endings. Way back in

1990 a baby girl was born on a British Airways flight from Ghana to London. Her mum called her Shona Kirsty Yves – or SKY. Fast-forward to 2016 and a baby boy got free flights for life from Libya-based Buraq Air when he arrived mid-flight – and was subsequently named after the plane's captain.

More recently the crew on Turkish Airlines had an unexpected arrival on their Boeing 737 in April 2017 when baby Kadiju joined the passenger list soon after take-off on a flight to Istanbul from Conakry in Guinea.

IS THERE A DOCTOR ON BOARD?

As I've already said, the cabin crew on your flight will be medically trained – and will have access to all sorts of medical kit in an emergency. But the good news is that we don't always have to tackle really serious problems on our own. When there's an 'Is there a doctor on board?' announcement then a lot of people normally come forward. Surveys show doctors tend to be very frequent fliers – they're well paid people so they take plenty of holidays and lots of them fly off to various medical conferences and research events as well. So statistically speaking most flights should have a scattering of doctors on board, as well as a fair few nurses, midwives and other medical professionals.

Dr Ben MacFarlane, author of the best-selling travelling doctor book *Holiday SOS*, tells of a time he was flying to a ski trip with a big group of friends from his medical school days. 'The call came out from the flight deck: Is there a doctor on board? My friend pushed the call button. "We've got three family doctors, two gastroenterologists, two anaesthetists, a paediatrician an oncologist and two clinical psychologists. Can you be a bit more specific about what you need?" she asked.'

Joking aside technology helps as well. Most airlines pay to have live links to medical facilities on the ground. Teams of doctors are based in places like MedAire in Phoenix, Arizona are standing by ready to talk crew or doctors step-by-step through the procedures they should follow if required. Pooling all the information and expertise together should allow sick passengers to be treated effectively – and for decisions to be made about emergency diversions if required. No-one ever wants planes to land anywhere other than their intended destination. But when medical situations require it, the flight deck crew will radio ahead to the nearest safe place to touch down and make sure an ambulance is waiting on the tarmac for the at-risk passenger.

Of course it is normally bad news for everyone else on board if you do need to head back down after a medical emergency. If the unscheduled stop comes early in a long-haul flight then the plane may have to ditch a lot of fuel (which I talk about elsewhere) before it lands. That means it will obviously need to re-fuel before continuing with the trip – and refuelling can take quite a while. To make matters worse, it can push the crew 'out of hours'.

Safety rules mean crew are only allowed to be on duty for a certain length of time – any longer and we'll be more like zombies or automatons than normal. If we go out of hours at our home base there should be a standby crew available to take over the flight so everyone gets on their way relatively quickly. But if we go out of hours elsewhere, which normally happens after a medical evacuation, then we need to have a set number of hours rest in a hotel before we're allowed to fly again. The only good news is that if we're in a hotel, you should be in a hotel too. Though do please note that I use the word 'should' rather than 'will' here. Logistics (and budgets) mean you might be pacing some foreign terminal waiting for a new boarding time to flash up on the departure boards. Sorry.

CAN YOU GET SUNBURN THROUGH A PLANE WINDOW?

Yes you can. And pilots often do (they're more at risk because the windows are far bigger in the cockpit) and recent research shows pilots have a significantly above average chance of suffering skin cancer. Because this is suddenly in the news I fly with plenty of flight deck crew who now put sun cream on their arms, faces and heads before they get on board.

Those of us in the rest of the plane are at less risk – though obviously anyone in a window seat is in more danger. As we're around six miles closer to the sun at cruising altitude, medics say that an hour of sun on your arm up at 35,000 feet is like spending 20 minutes in an electric sun bed.

The plane windows do stop UVB rays from getting to us. But they don't stop UVA rays, and these can be more dangerous. They're the ones that can trigger wrinkles, skin aging and skin cancer. Add that to the effect of dehydration and you'll see why it's worth putting some cream on as you settle into a window seat. If only to stop you looking a little one-sided when you reach your destination.

SHOULD YOU FLY WHEN YOU'VE GOT A COLD?

Doctors tell me it doesn't really matter – though passengers hate having to sit next to someone who sniffs or coughs for 12 straight hours so anything you can do to mask your symptoms will make everyone happier. But remember the first rule of medical aviation that says never to try medicine on a plane that you've never had on the ground. Six miles up is never a good place to discover you have an allergic reaction to a new drug. But as long as you've had decongestants before they are worth having to reduce the chance of severe ear pain on take-off and landing.

Ear pain happens when you can't balance out the pressure in your middle ear – as the air thins and thickens at the start and end of flights you need to equalise the pressure through your ear drum. But if your middle ear, the Eustachian tube, is swollen or blocked with cold-related mucus then that equalisation may not happen. And you'll feel it a lot more than normal on take-off and landing. Hence the call for decongestants. Other than that, something to ease your throat or stop your coughs and headaches can be fine. And while it's probably too late to help, I know lots of doctors who take a big dose of Vitamin C in the airport terminal to keep their systems topped up for the duration of the flight.

Fly to the Far East, in particular, and you'll often see passengers on board wearing those surgical masks. At first I thought people wore the masks to stop them getting colds from us (even though I'm told the masks are very unlikely to do this). But Far Eastern passengers tell me that most of them actually wear them out of kindness – they want to try and stop passing on their colds to others, which is nice (though, again, I'm told it's far from guaranteed to work).

And plane makers do try to stop germs getting around. Boeing filters claim to capture and remove between 94 and 99.9 per cent of airborne microbes, bacteria and even fungi, with a whole plane's air filtered and re-circulated every two to three minutes. That's something we don't get on the ground in a shop, an office, a cinema or any other popular place. So that's why some people think we're less rather than more likely to catch a cold on a plane.

Doctors who specialise in travel and travellers also say it pays to direct an overhead air jet towards you, if there is one. If the draft is annoying, they say to aim it just ahead of your face. The medics say the air coming directly from the air con system is likely to the cleanest on the plane – and that it can blow other peoples' germs away from you.

Finally, to boost your odds even more, remember a key rule of aviation medicine. Wash your hands as often as you can. Doctors say we're far more likely to catch a cold (or some other nasty) by touching an infected surface than by breathing in bad air. Hand sanitisers are worth using. And the new trend of using a dry, clean paper towel to touch the lock, flush button and taps in the plane toilet does seem to make sense to me.

WHY DO I FEEL BLOATED WHEN I FLY – AND WHAT CAN I DO ABOUT IT?

It's all to do with pressure – and a great Danish doctor called Jacob Rosenberg is very good at explaining it. He first got interested when he flew a lot, looked down, and thought his flat stomach was puffing out and looked a little less impressive at cruising altitude. He also watched an empty water bottle expand and contract as his plane went up and down on various flights.

'Since then I've noticed how much flatulence you have on a flight. Which is very much,' he concluded.

Basically when you're in the low pressure environment we create at 35,000 feet any air inside you expands into a bigger space. And whatever we say or think, we all have air inside us. In a typical day on land Rosenberg says we pass wind about ten times a day, letting rip around a litre of gas every 24 hours. And that litre of gas will need about a third more space when we're flying – so that's why our stomachs look bigger and feel a lot less comfortable.

One bit of advice to keep your bloating under control is to avoid carbonated drinks. Sparkling water, diet coke, tonic water and fizzy drinks take more air into your system. More air that can expand at altitude.

And once you get bloated, the simplest solution is to pass wind and let some of that pressure out. And the good news is that planes are equipped with charcoal filters to try and make that less uncomfortable for those around you. Boeing says the air on a plane is fully recirculated (having been through those vital filters) every two to three minutes. Airbus swears by its ozone removers as well.

To make things even better, there are extra air vents in most plane toilets as well - though these can still get very whiffy. If you're in a queue for the loo then cabin crew advice is always to take a moment (and possibly a deep breath) before going in. Opening the door as wide as possible before going in can help bad air move and dissipate just a little bit as well.

Last but not least you can do what cabin crew legend tells us about: crop dusting. It's when bloated crew walk fast from the front to the back of a plane, letting go as we do. We're crop-dusting and we disappear down the aisle before anyone notices what we've left in our wake.

IS IT SAFE TO TAKE SLEEPING PILLS WHEN YOU FLY?

Lots of people do. Plenty say it's the only way they can get through a long flight. But doctor friends give some words of warning. First up – remember the warning not to take a pill on a plane that you've never taken on land. As I said before, being six miles up and half way across an ocean in an aluminium tube is not an ideal place to discover you are allergic to one of the pill's ingredients. Some crew argue against taking sleeping pills as they don't like the thought that passengers may be groggy and slower than normal in an emergency. If we lose altitude fast, or even go for an unplanned landing, then we want everyone to have their wits about them.

Sleep experts also say that it's not really the noise or the activity that stops us from sleeping on planes. It's the low level pain we feel in different parts of our body because we're squashed in oddly shaped seats, rather than lying on a lovely flat bed. So they say simple painkillers can do just as much to help us nod off as full-scale sleeping pills.

It's also worth noting that doctors don't recommend taking antihistamines as 'sleeping pill substitutes' – especially for children. For while they normally make people drowsy, studies show that in the air they can have the opposite effect and make us hyper. Antihistamines can also depress our breathing a bit, and this can make it even harder to cope with the lower oxygen pressure we get at 35,000 feet.

HOW CAN I STOP MY EARS POPPING ON TAKE-OFF OR LANDING – AND SHOULD I FLY IF I'VE GOT EAR-ACHE?

Our ears pop as the cabin pressure changes as we ascend or descend to or from our cruising altitude – *Holiday SOS* author and travel doctor Ben MacFarlane tells me ear drums are actually really sensitive organs and changes to the whole ear canal inside our skull are what trigger motion or travel sickness.

As I've written elsewhere we're more likely to get ear pain if we fly with a cold – because congestion and mucus in our ears block the equalisation of pressure we need on take-off and landing. Some say it might help to use ear wax removal a few weeks before a flight, again to help the very sensitive ear membrane do its job unimpeded. But trying to remove ear wax with cotton buds is a big no. If you damage your ear drum doing this you'll make things even worse – and potentially quite dangerous. Once again simple painkillers (as long as you've taken them before and aren't allergic to them) are worth taking an hour before take-off and landing.

Ear-ache itself tends to be more common in children and babies than in adults – their ear canals are smaller and more sensitive and it's harder to get the message through to them that swallowing and yawning can help balance out the pressure and stop the pain.

Which reminds me of the old joke about a new crew member being a little bit blond (that applies to both sexes) when a passenger asked if she could ignore the Fasten Seat Belt sign and stand up quickly to get her bag out of the overhead locker. 'It's so I can get some chewing gum for my daughter's ears,' she told the crew member.

'Why do you want to put chewing gum in your daughter's ears?' he asked her, blondly.

The best ways to avoid ear pain include swallowing softly, then harder, then softly, then harder a few times as we go up or down.

Yawning, especially if you sort of wiggle your jaw and mouth around a bit as you do it, is good as well. Chewing gum or sucking a sweet can help too – as can laughing. Watch a comedy on the in-flight entertainment (or a horror film as a quick gasp of shock can also re-set your ears) and you might have a far smoother flight.

IS COFFEE AND TEA A HEALTH RISK ON PLANES?

This is something that we're being asked more and more nowadays. It didn't used to be a question at all – but social media seems to have given it some traction lately. People say it's because the hot water the crew use for the tea and coffee comes from big tanks in the plane – tanks that are rarely if ever properly cleaned. Worriers say that the tanks can therefore be full of bacteria and other nasties – so you should only ever drink bottled water or booze and drinks that come in a can.

Actual evidence on this is hard to find. And logic suggests it's not a problem. If I'm working in economy I can easily serve 400 cups of tea and coffee on a long-haul flight. If any of those drinkers got a stomach bug it would be me who'd have to help clean the toilets afterwards. So I'd know about it. And it just doesn't happen. And can bacteria actually get into a water tank in the first place? And don't things like coffee vending machines in offices have hard to reach and clean water tanks in them as well? When did any of us last clean the water in our kettles at home? Or the water bottles we take to the gym?

I'm happy to be told otherwise – and I appreciate that the water we use in the tea and coffee pots is hot, but not actually boiling (and even if it were to boil, the boiling point is lower at altitude than it is on the ground anyway). But I say the idea of water being a major health risk on planes is an urban myth. Flying is a long, tiring job – and next time you see a crew member in a plane galley he or she will almost certainly be drinking yet another black coffee.

I'M AFRAID OF FLYING. WHAT CAN I DO?

You can start off by remembering one key fact. Statistically speaking by the time you get on board your plane the most dangerous part of your whole day has already passed. All the figures show you are far more likely to be hurt or killed in a car on your way to the airport than you ever are on a plane. They also show you're far more likely to be injured tripping over the airplane step when you get off than you were in any mid-air emergency along the way.

A pilot also told me once that there are more than 20,000 planes up in the air at any given moment. That's tens of thousands of planes, 24 hours a day, seven days a week and 365 days a year. And news stories of problems are few and far between. 'Being involved in a plane crash is like walking into a vast room with several million people – and expecting the person in charge to pull your name out of a very, very large hat,' I've been told. Statistically it just isn't likely to happen.

But I totally get that people worry. We see them, when we stand at the plane doors for greet-and-seat. Pale faces, scared eyes, short breaths. There are so many nervous flyers out there that the condition has a name. It's aviophobia (oddly, something that sounds similar, aerophobia can also include fear of winds, drafts and even fresh air). But aviophobia breaks down into a host of different basic fears, not just of crashing and dying, but including fears of the unknown, claustrophobia and the dread of being out of control. Fortunately cabin crew are trained to help. Tell us you're nervous and we'll try to reassure you and watch over you a bit more.

Some people swear by hypnotherapy – and there are all sorts of books and audio programmes that can see you through the problem as well. Others say that people's real fear tends to be loss of control – we don't like that whatever happens is out of our hands. So experts suggest focusing on decisions you can make, things you can control, to overcome the worries. Mapping out a flight. Saying: I'm going to watch this film. Then I'm going to ask for a cup of coffee. Then I'm going to read five chapters in my book. Then I'm going to watch that film. Experts say a simple strategy like that can really help. Puzzles, long books or any other distractions are worth having too.

If your fears are really strong then some swear by courses. Several airlines offer sessions, run by pilots and cabin crew, where you can hear the truth about how safe planes are, you can sit in mock-up cabins and hear good self-help strategies so you feel more at home in the real thing. And the last thing nervous flyers should do? Drink. Dutch courage in the terminal or the air really won't help. As crew, whenever we see nervous flyers knock back the booze we know they're going to feel worse, not better. We see it every day.

HOW MUCH ALCOHOL CAN I DRINK ON A FLIGHT?

It depends on the airline. If you have to pay for drinks, and your cabin crew get commission on every passenger purchase, then I'd say 'drink as much as you can afford'. If drinks are free then you might also think there's no limit. But there are limits, of course, and again it's all down to safety. I've got cabin crew friends who get really annoyed at how much some passengers try to drink on board. 'It's a plane, not a nightclub' they say. And just like nightclubs, the last thing we want to see around us are drunks.

In the olden days you could expect to be told enough is enough once you started getting loud and unsteady. Nowadays we don't even want things to get this far. Cabin crew are trained in recognising and dealing with drunks. And airlines are a lot less generous than they used to be anyway. We carry less bottles on board than we did a few years ago. Booze is heavy and heavy planes cost more to fly around. So we really do run out sooner than we did. Some crew are more assertive than others when it comes to saying no to repeated requests for drink. But don't assume you can play one of us off against another. As soon as we flag up a passenger as on the edge we pass it on. So don't think I don't know how many Jack Daniels and Coke my colleagues have already served you in the other galley. Don't think I'll believe it if you say the second red wine is for your wife.

Finally, don't think you can beat the system by drinking your own booze on board. That bottle of vodka you bought in the terminal? It's illegal to drink your own alcohol on a plane. If we suspect it we can investigate – asking your neighbours and looking for evidence, like, oh I don't know, half empty vodka bottles under your seat. We can get the Captain involved – they normally love a bit of this – and after recording that you've been handed pre-printed warnings we can start the whole process that leads to fines and even possible prosecution on the ground.

Last off all there's the obvious warning. The body doesn't really like alcohol under pressure in the dry, dehydrating air of planes. Drink too much in the sky and you get a heck of a hangover on land. One unit of alcohol in the sky is said to pack the same punch as two or even three on the ground. Getting a hangover towards the end of a long flight is not a good way to start a holiday, a business trip or to face up to real life on your return.

BUT I CAN TANK UP ON BOOZE IN THE TERMINAL, RIGHT?

Wrong – just ask David Hasslehoff who was seen staggering around the First Class lounge at London's Heathrow airport way back in 2006 before trying to join his British Airways flight to Los Angeles. He was deemed too drunk to fly. So he didn't fly.

Since then staff in airport bars and restaurants are told and trained to stop serving people before they tip over the edge, or tip off the edge of a bar stool (though as the companies want to make profits and the staff want to make tips I'm never sure how tough they really are). But the people at the boarding gates should be a lot more vigilant. Holding a ticket and a boarding pass does not guarantee you a seat on your plane. Nor does making it to your seat. If the cabin crew are concerned about you then they'll have a word. If things get heated then the captain will come out of the cockpit to test the air. If he or she thinks there's any chance you might endanger the aircraft, or endanger yourself or others by being disruptive or being unable to exit fast in an emergency, then you'll be sent back to the terminal.

Refuse to leave the plane and we'll radio the police in the terminal and they'll happily hop on board to make you change your mind. Oh, and while you should get the chance to sober up in the terminal and then switch on to a later flight there is no actual obligation on an airline to let you fly on its next flight. So you could end up having to buy a whole new and very expensive last minute ticket for a rival.

Finally, don't forget that the alcohol you drink on a plane doesn't magically disappear when you land. If you're getting into a rental car, or picking up your own car, straight after arrivals, then think back to how much you did drink on board. Driving a car when you're over-tired, jet-lagged, disoriented and still even slightly drunk is unlikely to end well.

CAN I SMOKE E-CIGARETTES ON BOARD?

Airlines have taken a while to get to grips with this one – but the answer is pretty much no, partly because of the vapour that e-cigarettes can produce. Seeing what looks like a cloud of smoke rise up in the cabin will make passengers and your cabin crew incredibly nervous. So in most cases – and if your airline has faced up to the fact that e-cigarettes exist and written a policy – then they're banned.

And don't think you can sneak off to the privacy of the toilet with your e-cigarette. Most smoke detectors will sense them as well – so the alarms will go off and we'll come knocking on the door to investigate. Get caught breaking the rules here and it can cost you more than the embarrassment of walking back to your seat in front of a full, disapproving cabin of fellow passengers. Arline policies differ and they may offer warnings rather than maximum penalties. But worst case scenario can see you taken to court, fined heavily and banned from your airline for life.

Disabling the smoke detectors is equally off limits – and disabling includes trying to cover them up or stuffing paper over them to stop the smoke hitting the sensor. The latest ones, on the newest planes, have even started to go off if you squirt too much perfume in the lav when you're sprucing yourself up for landing.

But back to e-cigarettes. The complicated, potentially frustrating and slightly unusual extra thing about them is that while you're not allowed to use them in a flight, you will probably have to bring them on board with you. Because most e-cigarette machines contain potentially flammable lithium batteries (Samsung's Galaxy Note 7, anyone?) they're not allowed to go in checked bags in the hold. This kind of information gets updated all the time, obviously. So check online or at check-in before you fly.

HOW SOON CAN YOU FLY AFTER SURGERY?

Obviously you want to confirm this with your own doctor, who will know your exact circumstances. Generally speaking it will also depend on the type of surgery you've had. Anything abdominal needs a longer wait, because with this kind of surgery air can get into parts of our body where it isn't normally found. It will gradually get absorbed away. But while it's there, in an abdominal cavity, for example, it risks expanding when we reach the thin air of our cruising altitude. The expansion can be painful, dangerous and even burst some of the stitches that are repairing the wound.

Doctors say common operations like hip surgery are less likely to trigger airborne complications – though there can be other problems caused by sitting still for long periods so people with medical issues should try to move around as much as possible. Doctors say you should be fine to fly after dental surgery, though again tiny pockets of air in a tooth can be painful if it expands at altitude.

Other stitches in wounds shouldn't be affected by pressure changes or flying, though dry air can cause itching. Plastic surgery like nose jobs doesn't rule you out of flying – and we do see lots of passengers with suspicious black eyes heading back to Europe from Brazil, for example, where some of the world's best plastic surgeons work.

CAN YOU FLY WITH A BROKEN ARM OR LEG?

If your arm or leg is in a cast then best advice is to get the cast broken before you fly. If you don't and your limb swells it's going to be incredibly painful and can push back your recovery. You can have your limb bandaged up so it stays immobile for the flight, though it shouldn't be too tight as you don't want to cut off your blood circulation. So some extra give for potential swelling will help. Then have a new cast put on as soon as possible when you get to your destination. And on the flight take care you don't make matters worse by bashing into anyone, or being in a position where a person, or a trolley, can bash into you.

Can you expect a lovely upgrade to Business or First Class if you turn up bandaged up looking like The Mummy? Unfortunately not (not least as we do get burned by people with fake injuries who will do anything to get out of the zoo in economy). But we will try to help you get around the cabin, and pay more attention to keeping you hydrated and happy if you're less able than most to get up and about yourself.

IS IT RIGHT YOU CAN'T FLY AFTER SCUBA-DIVING?

You do need to wait long enough to ensure you won't effectively get 'the bends' on your flight. When you dive you go deep under water and put your body under massive unexpected pressure. You also breathe air from a compressed canister on your back – air that contains a higher percentage of oxygen and nitrogen than we breathe in day to day life. Under pressure, below the ocean, the nitrogen dissolves in your blood – and all being well it will gradually leak out of your body (mainly through urine) in the hours and days after your dive.

But if you get into a plane before that extra nitrogen has dissipated, then at the lower pressure levels of cruising altitude the nitrogen can form bubbles in your blood or some body tissues (it's a bit like opening a can of coke after shaking it). The bubbles can do real damage right across your body. They can cause muscle or joint pain, headaches, fatigue and sudden rashes in the best case scenarios. And they can cut off the blood supply to your brain, in some of the worst ones.

Most dive experts say you should wait 24 hours after your last dive before you fly. Some more cautious people suggest as long as 48 hours. Fly too soon and you can need to be put in a hyperbaric oxygen chamber to push the nitrogen back into your blood so it can leak out of your body in the normal way.

Finally, it's not just flying that you need to watch out for after scuba dives. The doctors I spoke to warn against hot tubs and alcohol – and mountain climbing. Go to Hawaii to dive in the morning and climb a volcano at night and you can face the same issues that you'd face if you flew too soon after scuba.

WHAT HAPPENS IF SOMEONE DIES ON A PLANE?

Statistically speaking it's bound to happen every now and then. They estimate that more than 3 billion flights are taken every year – that's more than 8 million people flying every day. Many will be there for ten, twelve or more hours. Lots of older people travel. And, of course, ill people travel, maybe to get to countries with better hospitals or maybe to get closer to loved ones for their final days.

So yes, people will die. But planes don't have coffins or morgues at the back or under the floor. I'm always amazed how many people think we do. I'm amazed how often I get asked: 'Where's the coffin cupboard?' as if such a thing exists and every inch of space on a plane isn't already allocated for things we need right now.

So as a rule of thumb, if someone dies in their seat they may well stay there. Cabin crew are jokers and we make light of a lot of things. But we get serious and try to treat people with respect when it counts. So we don't want to lift, drag or otherwise manhandle a lost loved one across a cabin. Nor do we want other passengers to see this. If someone has died we want to keep things as discrete and low key as we can. I've read other people say that dead passengers 'will probably be moved to First Class'. Not on any plane I've ever flown. Drag a corpse up the aisle and through the curtains of economy and business class? It's never going to happen because it's not the corpse we'll move if the worst happens. If you're not travelling with the lost passenger, or if you're a loved one who doesn't want to stay alongside them, then we might try to move you to First or to a spare seat elsewhere in the plane. But generally speaking we'll leave a dead passenger where they are.

If you've somehow slept through the activity that has gone on alongside a death, we will wake you to try to move you. There was a terrible (though maybe unfairly exaggerated) story from 2007 when a man in one of the premium cabins of a British Airways flight from Delhi to London woke up to find a dead passenger being moved into the seat across the aisle from him. He said the crew didn't explain things properly to him – though in their defence they said they were simply doing the best they could think to do in very difficult situations.

There was another scandal once about a crew allegedly putting a corpse in a plane toilet for landing. I do hope that never truly happened. Apart from basic humanity, it shouldn't for several reasons. There are no seatbelts in toilets, as I've mentioned before. So a body can get damaged if we hit turbulence. It can also move or fall to the floor, making it hard to open the door to remove the body undamaged when we're on the ground.

This next bit might be too much information, but crew are also trained to be ready for other things if passengers die. Bowels and bladders can relax after death – so we try to put blankets or other protective coverings underneath the corpse to protect the seat and the cabin floor.

There might also be dead bodies beneath the cabin floor, of course. Coffins are transported in the hold, in many cases. There's said to be an airline code that tells the crew if any corpses are on board: the official description is HR or Human Remains but an urban myth says the phrase 'Jim Wilson is on board' is used as another way of saying 'there's a coffin in the hold'. I've never heard the

117

phrase myself. Cabin crew don't get access to the hold – you can't climb into it from anywhere I know on a plane. So we've no reason to know what might be in it on any given flight.

Lastly, it's an interesting fact that having said all this, some argue that no-one ever does actually die in the air. I'm told death hasn't legally happened until it's been certified to have happened by a health or legal professional on the ground. Ben MacFarlane, the travel doctor and author of one of my favourite books, *Holiday SOS* tells of the time he was kept away from a clearly dead fellow passenger and told the man was 'sleeping'. 'They said it was because there was less paperwork if the death note was issued on the ground so I was firmly guided back to my seat and told I'd be called back if the man "woke up",' he says.

SHOULD YOU TAKE YOUR CONTACT LENSES OUT WHEN YOU FLY?

Lots of people do. Plane air is a lot drier than ordinary air – its humidity levels can be between 12 and 20 per cent, which is drier than you get in many deserts. Planes could improve this, but it would cost a huge amount to bring the right sort of humidifying equipment on board. Plus the weight of the extra water we'd have to carry would probably get passed on through higher ticket prices. Making cabins far more humid would bring other problems – including speeding up the corrosion of vital parts of the fuselage, which no-one really wants. It can also cause 'cabin rain' – when sudden pressure changes trigger a sudden 'dew point' and the moisture in the air falls down on all our heads.

Opticians say dry contact lenses can, in the worst cases, scratch the surface of our eyes. So they recommend using eye drops every now and then if you do keep your lenses in. If you take them out, they say the other risk is the one I've talked about before: contamination. Once you've touched everything from your tray table, to the seat backs around you, to the toilet door and the toilet lock you really don't want to touch your eyes. So best advice is to really take care washing your hands before removing your lenses. Or take them out, and put them in again, in the terminal at the start and at the end of your flight.

CAN YOU BE TOO FAT TO FLY?

This is becoming a real issue as we all seem to eat more and get ever larger. Three basic factors come into play. First, can you get into the seat? Second, can you get a seat belt around you? Third, what will it mean for your neighbour?

If you can't get into one seat – and if the arm rest between seats goes up fully – then you might be able to book and pay for two. That's what the writer, comedian and *Clerks* director Kevin Smith did in 2010 when he followed airline policy and booked two seats on a Southwest Airlines flight from northern to southern California. Unfortunately it didn't quite work out, because when he was given the chance to move on to an earlier flight, where there was only one spare seat, there were issues about him fitting into it. After a little debate he was asked to leave that full plane and return for his original departure time – appearing to prove that you really could be too fat to fly.

Fortunately the seat belt issue is easily solved. All flights should carry extension seat-belts – which pretty much work the way they sound. They attach to the existing belt to almost double its length so larger people can still say safe. Handing them out can be tricky – we really won't want to embarrass people. No-one I worked with ever yelled out: 'We need a fat belt in Row 33' to a colleague. If we think you might need an extension we'll offer it. If we don't offer, then just attract our attention before take-off and ask.

Oh, and do you know who the crew love? People who hand extension belts back at the end of a flight. Just bringing yours to the front of the plane and telling the crew you've left it on the first row of seats up there makes everyone's life easier. It means we don't have to twist and turn looking around and under seats to find it when we've got a tight turnaround and just want to get the next flight out on time.

And the passengers next to you? This is tricky. In an ideal world we'd all have an empty seat next to us, or at worst a tiny, bird-like and silent elderly lady. Get someone whose body mass encroaches over the arm-rest into our space and the flight will be a lot less fun. Best advice is to try to be discrete and charming. Go to the galley as soon as you can – during boarding if possible – and explain the situation calmly and politely. Ask if there's anywhere else you could be moved to. If you're unpleasant about it we won't help and you'll be stuck where you are. But if we like you, we'll probably take pity on you. And if it's possible to move you elsewhere we will.

Lastly, I should turn the question around and admit that in the past airlines have decreed that their staff could be too fat to fly. For a while, crew were recruited on the basis of talent – stewards tended to be ex-army while the first female attendants were ex-nurses. Then it all got a sexist and look-ist.

When the old Pan Am started to fly women could only apply to be flight attendants (called air hostesses) if they were unmarried, at least 5 foot 2 tall, weighed no more than 130 lbs and had no children. Their weight was regularly monitored – not least as you were never allowed a larger uniform size than the one you were originally issued. Oh, and women had to retire at 32, when the airline thought they would look too old to fly. More amazing than this, really, is that the retirement age rule lasted till the 1970s, the unmarried rule till the 1980s and the weight rule till the 1990s!

If you want to see the ultimate in old-fashioned sexism type 'British Airways Sergeant Major advert' into YouTube and you won't quite believe how things used to be.

HOW DANGEROUS IS DVT?

It is serious, and it's great that passengers focus on it far more than before. Deep Vein Thrombosis happens when a clot, a thrombosis, forms in a deep vein, often the ones in the calf muscles of our legs. If the clot then breaks off it can travel around the bloodstream and create a blockage. The real danger is that the blockage happens at the lungs, stopping blood getting from the heart to the lungs where it loads up with oxygen. This triggers a pulmonary embolism, which can kill.

DVT can happen in all sorts of places, not just on planes. People can get it sitting still for too long in a car, coach or train. You can even start to develop it by sitting at a desk or in a cinema for too long. But doctors think several factors make it more likely to suffer DVT on a plane – not least the cramped conditions and the sheer length of some transcontinental journeys.

The first bit of prevention advice is to stay mobile. However much it may annoy your neighbours if you've got a window seat then get up every half hour or so (at least every hour) and walk up and down the aisle. Stretch a bit in the space outside the toilets, perhaps – letting others go ahead as the longer you stand there with blood pumping through your body the better. When you're sitting it's important to move your legs as much as you can. Most in-flight magazines, and some of the TV channels, have 'wellbeing' sections that give you tips. But moving any part of your leg, but especially the feet and lower leg, will help blood get pumped through it and reduce the chance of a clot forming.

Good advice is to stay hydrated as well. Dehydration can be a trigger for the start of DVT – and everything about travel can lead to unusual amounts of dehydration. If you were late for your flight, if you got stressed and ran sweating across the terminal (after ditching your water bottle at security) then try to buy more water before you get on the plane.

Most crew take an empty water bottle through security, then fill it up airside where there are normally water fountains by the toilets. Once on board order water, no ice – that gets more into you cup, believe it or not. Alcohol, tea and coffee are all supposed to be diuretics – they dehydrate our bodies, effectively taking more water out than they put in. So the experts advise against too much of them on board. Regular sips of water, from your own bottle, alongside the exercises and movement are a great prevention strategy.

Doctors say the jury is out on flight socks – the ones that are supposed to hold our leg muscles together and encourage blood to flow rather than clot. But while few doctors are prepared to say for certain that the socks help, even fewer have ever said they could do any harm. So there's probably no reason not to try them.

Taking aspirin before flights is another grey area. In theory it thins the blood, and helps stop clots forming. But it can have side effects (lots of medical conditions mean you shouldn't take aspirin, and again you should never try something you've not had before, or not for a long time, on a flight). People who think aspirin can help suggest taking a small amount every day a week or so before you take a long flight. I had a lady on board once who had booked a surprise trip from London to New York for her husband's 70th birthday. She had ground down half an aspirin pill every morning for a week and put it in his orange juice. But as medical opinion can change on this all the time it's important to do your own research –

and to speak to your own doctor – before you self-medicate, even with aspirin.

If you do fall prey to DVT you're likely to feel it in your legs first – though it can start elsewhere as well. Signs include redness, swelling, warmth and fatter veins. If DVT gets to the next stage, of a pulmonary embolism, there's pain, breathlessness and dizziness among other symptoms – and you should get help fast.

If you have concerns it's always worth speaking to a doctor before you fly. If you start to worry on board then speak to a member of crew. As I've said elsewhere in the book, we can almost always find a doctor on the plane. And we can link up to qualified aviation doctors on the ground as well for extra advice.

Finally, it's worth remembering that DVT issues don't always become apparent on or straight after a flight. Doctors say it can take several days for any symptoms to show up. So stay alert – and stay hydrated and mobile after your flight as well. Arriving in a hot, holiday destination and failing to drink much water can make a bad situation worse. Doctors say that if your first purchase at your destination is a bottle of water then you're doing the right thing.

WHAT IF I NEED EXTRA OXYGEN DURING A FLIGHT?

We're seeing more and more people travelling with tough medical needs – including those with conditions like Chronic Obstructive Pulmonary Disease or COPD. If you're one of them it's obviously important to tell your doctor you are travelling – and get advice. Tests can work out how well you're likely to cope with the lower pressure air at altitude and you may be advised to have some emergency medications to guard against things like lung infections. As with all medications it's important to put them in your hand luggage, not your checked bags.

Different airlines have different policies regarding getting and using extra oxygen on board. Portable Oxygen Concentrators can often be hired by partner companies – though they can't always be provided last minute. Best advice is to arrange one when you book, or as far before your flight as possible.

If you want to plug into our extra oxygen on board you'll again have to get permission beforehand, so contact your airline as early as possible. You'll have to pay for an extra on-board canister - fees can be hundreds of pounds or dollars. You'll probably need a medical note as well saying why you need the extra help. And check if you need to bring your own oxygen mask or cannula – not every airline supplies them.

Whatever you do, your crew should have been told you're coming, and where you're sitting. But obviously a polite reminder on boarding won't go amiss. And it's not just oxygen where extra efforts are made for people with health issues. As well as wheelchair assistance in terminals most long-haul airlines have special, thinner wheel-chairs that can fit down airline aisles (they're often called aisle-chairs) and crew know which on-board toilets have wider or easy opening doors – because not every toilet on a plane is exactly alike.

HOW DO YOU BEAT JET LAG?

Cabin crew talk about this more than almost anything else. There are hundreds of theories and it's clear that different strategies work for different people. It's also worth noting that jet lag hits worse when you fly east. So heading from London to Singapore, or from

Los Angeles to Paris, is going to wipe you out more than flying the other way. West is best, East is a beast, any cabin crew member will tell you.

And don't just think that jet lag is about feeling exhausted and lying awake ridiculously long in your hotel or home bed. Indigestion, constipation, loss of appetite, memory and focus are all signs of jet lag.

One jet lag beating trick is to prepare for your new time zone in advance. If you're flying west then stay up a few hours later every night in the week before your trip. If you're flying east, then go to bed an hour or so earlier than normal in the days before you fly.

Lots of people swear by putting yourself on 'destination time' as soon as you get on your plane. But I'm never sure that really always works. If it's a bright and sunny 9am in London and you're off to Las Vegas it's hard to live as if it's 1am in the desert. We'll be serving lunch, as we start off our meals on local time, while you'll be wanting an early breakfast if you're already in Vegas mode. My advice is to just ride with it till the final quarter of your flight. Then get on to Vegas time. Airline policy varies, but most move onto destination mode at this point, so we will serve breakfast now, to match local time.

When you're on board it helps to say no to alcohol – and to cut down on tea and coffee. You might think a few glasses of wine might help you sleep but jet lag combined with a hangover is not a pleasure. Dehydration combined with jet lag is no fun either – and as I've said elsewhere, tea and coffee can take more moisture out of you than they put in. Getting a caffeine fix when your body clock is already haywire can also make a bad job worse. Ditto sleeping pills. Take some on board and get some sleep when your body is totally confused about where and what time it is, and you can stay out of whack for longer at your destination.

For my money the most important thing to do next is to forget all about what time it is at home. Live entirely, and fully, in local time. Don't even join in any conversations about: 'Wow, it's midnight back home' or anything like that. This just further confuses your brain and your body. Try to stay up and go through the whole day as normal. If you feel rough, just treat it as if you had noisy neighbours or a crying baby and didn't get much sleep at home. Get out and about as much as possible. Fresh air and, crucially, sunshine can re-set your body clock – though there's a trick here as well. If you're going west then go out into the fresh air and natural light in the morning, and then try to avoid the sun in the afternoon. If you've gone east, then stay in the shadows in the morning and go out and get some natural or sun light in the afternoon.

In both cases, go to bed early, but not ridiculously early. And then, as I say, continue to live 100 per cent in local time.

Do cat naps help, especially if you've flown east? They can do. But if you make them too long you may not sleep at night which pushes things out of line for longer.

Some colleagues swear by melatonin as a jet lag beater – but you don't need to spend long online to see that critics say they're being duped. It's a drug that effectively plays with our hormones, which never seems an entirely great thing to do. Some say it's also made up of dangerous bits from animals – dangerous bits we really shouldn't be ingesting. The drug is hard to come by in the UK, for example, as the authorities aren't sure about its safety or effectiveness. But it's easier to get (even in supermarkets) in the US. Lots of homeopathic pills are also on offer (as are expensive 'blue lamp' light remedies and other so-called miracle cures) with little evidence that they actually work. But I've got one cabin crew friend who cheerfully admits that she likes the marketing and is the kind to fall for a placebo so she takes them and says they do the trick every time.

CHAPTER FOUR – Cabin Crew Secrets.

Sing or Dance - Borrowing pens - Bunk beds – Sleeping with the pilots – What's banned in the cockpit – When Tom Cruise is on board – What closed curtains mean – The First Class crews – Eye Drops if you're rude – The boys on the crew – The girls on the crew who marry well – Dinner for the captain – Pilots in glasses –Is My Plane A Racist? – Has It Got A Nickname? - Top tips from the crew – Crew as airheads – Lost property on planes – Friends on the crew – When cabin crew spill drinks – When cabin crew get to the layover hotel – Party time – The mile high club.

BEFORE TAKE-OFF ONE FLIGHT I OVERHEARD ONE CREW MEMBER ASK THE OTHER: DO YOU WANT TO SING OR DANCE? WHAT WAS THAT ALL ABOUT?

It was about what's known as 'the manual safety demonstration'. Lots of planes show safety videos on the seat back or ceiling television screens. When this happens you just need crew to be stationed at key points in the cabin to point out those vital nearest exits when the moment comes.

But when the safety videos can't be loaded for some reason, or on smaller or older planes that don't even have them, the crew have to do it another way. One person has to read out the words of the safety scripts (everything about seat belts, oxygen masks, life jackets and so on) – so in crew-talk that person 'sings'. Meanwhile the other crew member has to stand in front of the cabin demonstrating how all the kit works. That person 'dances'. So, 'Do you want to sing or dance?' it's up to the crew who does what. Some hate talking on the PA, so they opt to dance. Some hate standing in front of a hundred bored, disinterested or sometimes lecherous passengers, so they opt to sing.

WHY WON'T THE FLIGHT ATTENDANT LEND ME A PEN FOR MY IMMIGRATION FORM? THEY'VE GOT ONE IN THEIR SHIRT POCKET. WHY CAN'T I BORROW IT?

It sounds selfish but it's actually the law. Safety rules mean cabin crew are supposed to have pens on them at all times – and they're not supposed to hand them to anyone else in case they need them. In an emergency or special situation the captain or someone from the flight deck will call in the most senior cabin crew member on duty for a NITS briefing. NITS is the what, when, where and how of the situation – crew need to write it down so we can pass it on to our colleagues accurately. The 'N' is the Nature of the incident, a planned ditching in water, a diversion to an alternative airport for medical reasons or whatever it is. The 'I' is the Intention of the flight deck, to perform an emergency landing or whatever it is. The 'T' is the Time available, or the time the manoeuvre will begin. The 'S' is any Special Instructions.

Once he or she has repeated the NITS briefing back to the flight deck the cabin manager has to head to the cabin, get on the 'All Crew' phone and pass it on to every cabin crew member – who will also be writing the key facts down. These are not details we want to get wrong. This is not a time for us to be scratching around for a pen. That's why you can't have ours. Sorry.

IS IT TRUE THAT CABIN CREW HAVE 'SECRET' BUNK BEDS WHERE THEY CAN SLEEP DURING A FLIGHT?

It depends on the flight and the plane – but yes, when we get really lucky we do get somewhere special to sleep on board. And we do need it. Passengers don't realise that by the time they get greeted at the door of a plane the crew have been on duty for at least an hour. At our home base, we've uniformed up, gone through our own security line and sat in a pre-flight briefing, often facing a variety of random safety and medical questions to make sure we're on our toes. At a layover destination we would have got uniformed up in our hotel, have done the briefing in the lobby, then had what can be quite a long drive to the airport to join everyone else in security. That done, we probably boarded the plane half an hour before the first passenger so we can do all the pre-flight safety and other checks. Throw in a twelve hour, long-haul flying time and we'll want at least a bit of a break before we get to our destination.

So where do we sleep? We use a special key to open a secret Harry Potter style door to the crew rest area. It's a door you can walk past loads of times before you even notice it. Most of the time the crew rest is above the passenger cabin, so on the other side of the door there's a ladder going up. On other planes the rest area is below the main deck so the ladder takes us down.

Once inside you find yourself in a windowless room with half a dozen or so coffin-shaped beds. It's no place for people with claustrophobia. Nor is it a place to hang around if you're shy. We get curtains to pull across each bunk area to give us some privacy. But there's not much room in the bunk, so if people want to get their kit off they normally do it right there in the middle bit (hopefully with the trap door on top of the ladder closed so no-one falls down the hole in an upper-level rest area).

Cabin crew aren't known for their shy and retiring nature. What goes on in the bunk area normally proves that point pretty conclusively. And do some crew do more than just sleep in the bunks? There's not a lot of room for anything fun. But I have to tell you that on most planes two oxygen masks fall down into each single bunk in an emergency. Enough said.

AND DO THE PILOTS SLEEP WITH THE CABIN CREW, AS IT WERE?

Not on the plane. Though it has to be said that they do, very often, almost everywhere else. The flight deck crew get their own secret Harry Potter doors to their own sleeping quarters up at the front of the plane. Their rest rooms (in the literal sense) are smaller as there won't normally be more than three people up front and at least one of them has to be in the cockpit to fly the plane. The flight deck rest area is up front so it's closer to the cockpit in case there's an emergency and the senior officers need to be called back fast. And it's sometimes a little posher, as well. They can get their own private loo, on some planes, and mini arm-chairs as well as bunks.

Pilots can sleep on the flight deck as well – especially on smaller planes with fewer people in the cockpit and no actual bunk rooms to sneak off to. It's called 'controlled rest' in the cockpit (as opposed to bunk rest) and it's basically a power nap where one of the flight deck crew agrees with the other that he or she is going to belt up, push their chair back a bit from the controls and close their eyes for ten to thirty minutes. It only ever happens mid-cruise – never in the busy patches like take-off or landing – and it helps keep the pointy end crew fresh and alert for the rest of the flight.

But back to the other meaning of the question. Do the pilots sleep with the cabin crew? All the time. At least once a month I seem to fly with a flight deck/main deck married couple.

WHAT'S NOT ALLOWED IN THE COCKPIT?

I love this one. Obviously all sorts of things aren't allowed on the other side of reinforced cockpit doors. Elephants, for example. Or guns. Or working pole-dancers. But one of the more surprising items that's actually on written down banned substance lists? It's sugar.

If a captain or first officer wants a cup of tea or coffee with sugar then the sugar has to be put in and stirred out in the galley. Cabin crew can't put sugar sachets on the tray with a stirrer and take it up front for the flight deck crew to mix themselves.

Why? It's because sugar granules can do a lot of dangerous damage in the cockpit. If they spill over the instruments then the grains can get jammed in the switches and buttons and potentially stop them working when they're needed.

On the same note, cabin crew get equally important instructions for serving any type of flight deck drinks. If we're bringing something for the Captain, who sits on the left-hand side of the cockpit, we have to pass anything to them over his or her left shoulder – avoiding the main instrument panel in the middle. When we serve the First Officer, who sits on the right when they're both there, then we pass to the drink over his or her right shoulder, for the same reason.

AND WHY DID I HEAR CABIN CREW ASK IF TOM CRUISE IS ON BOARD?

Because they weren't talking about the film star. Tom Cruise is airline jargon for Tea and Coffee – and it just reminds us which identical silver pot contains which drink. If 'Tom Cruise is on board' we're following the standard pattern – tea pot on the left of the trolley, coffee pot on the right, so it's Tom Cruise as we look at them.

As a very obvious extra, if we're out on the drinks round and you see us go into a YMCA mode curving an arm into the vague shape of a big 'C' or putting one palm on top of our other fingers in the shape of a 'T' we're just telling our colleague in the galley which drink pot is running low and needs a refill. And if we squeeze our hand up and down and look borderline obscene we're mimicking milking a cow. We're telling colleagues in the galley we need a top up of milk.

WHY ARE ALL THE CURTAINS CLOSED ROUND THE EMERGENCY DOORS ON MY LONG-HAUL FLIGHT?

It's because some poor crew member is trying to bed down and get some sleep on a pile of cardboard boxes and newspapers on the other side of them. Not every plane has bunk rooms for crew breaks, as I've described earlier. And even if they do, not every crew member likes being packed in what look like coffins with their assorted colleagues. So we need other places to go for some rest on long flights.

Space, of course, is at a premium on every flight nowadays. If any extra space exists, the managers will put a passenger seat on it to make extra revenue. The one place they can't do that is in front of the emergency exit doors that run up the sides of a jumbo. So those few precious square feet of dirty carpet are where we try to spend a happy hour mid-flight. The jump seats along the side of the door do pull out slightly. And if there's a second jump seat facing the first you can often put a metal tray from the galley across between the two to try and make a makeshift bed.

It won't be very soft. And it will be cold, as the doors do let in drafts from the sub-zero degree air we're going through. So that's where the flattened out cardboard boxes and the old newspapers come in. We spread them on the floor or on the make-shift bed to make it softer and a tad more hygienic. 'As cabin crew we sleep in

133

doorways on piles of old newspapers. We're basically just one step up from homeless people,' as I was told on one of my first flights.

The other place we sometimes sleep if there are no bunks is the back row of economy. On some planes you'll see a tented-thing built back there – with another set of curtains pulled around the three or four seats in the middle of the cabin. Those seats will have been kept empty at boarding and they'll be blocked off for crew. The curtains are pulled round when the first crew break starts and we try to get some shut eye.

So one quick favour. If you do see the curtains closed anywhere on your next flight please leave us alone. Don't pull the curtains apart for a quick peek – that's just rude. And try to keep the noise down if you're near the curtains. Someone in charge of your safety – and your breakfast – is trying to recharge their batteries in a pretty uncomfortable place just a few feet away.

DO THE SAME CREW WORK IN FIRST CLASS OR IN ECONOMY ALL THE TIME? AND IF NOT HOW DO YOU DECIDE WHO WORKS WHERE?

It depends on the airline, but most crew find themselves in different cabins all the time. Some airlines allocate different cabins based on crew seniority – old timers get First or Business Class and newbies get economy or coach. But often there's an element of choice – the old timers get the choice while newbies work wherever is left. And what surprises friends is the fact that lots of crew actively choose to work at the back.

Some long-term crew I've worked with literally hate the premium cabins. They say the passengers up there are too demanding, too snooty and sometimes too rude. Others don't like working First Class, in particular, because the job and the service there is too fiddly and complicated. They say they prefer just flinging sandwiches about or handing over plastic trays in economy to dealing with white table cloths, proper place settings and fancy food service that's expected in First (where contrary to some reports we don't get paid more to work).

Clever crew members also look at the flight manifest before choosing where they work. If First Class is due to be choc full and economy is half empty then most of us would go for an easier life in economy. Some also prefer the back of the plane because it's more social. There are more crew back there and we're allowed to have a bit more fun. Privacy and discretion rule in the posh cabins up front.

With most airlines it's only the First Class crew who are allowed to walk through the velvet curtains to spend time in the galley up there – and the people there have to keep their voices down to avoid disturbing the big-spenders. At the back of the plane any of the rest of the crew can pop back for a gossip whenever they get a chance – so you can make a bit more noise and have a lot more fun.

That said, who's not going to like First Class if there's a hot celebrity up there? Or a potential rich husband or wife - cabin crew tend to marry richer than any other profession, after all? And with some airlines only a select bunch of crew get First Class training, so that seriously limits everyone's ability to choose.

IF YOU'RE RUDE TO CABIN CREW WILL THEY REALLY PUT EYE DROPS IN YOUR FOOD TO GIVE YOU THE RUNS?

That's one of the old stories that's been spread about nasty cabin crew for years. Of course we'd never do that. We're too nice. We're too kind. We're too professional and too well trained. Oh, and we're the people who have to do regular toilet checks throughout the flight. So if we give you the runs we'll be the ones clearing up afterwards. We'll also be in our jump seat right next to the smelly lavatory for landing. So eye-drops don't happen.

But trust me. If you're rude to us we will find some other way to make your flight a misery. Your extra diet coke almost certainly won't arrive. And if it does, the can may have been mysteriously shaken up ready to explode all over your clothes when you open it. And depending where you're sitting, your seat back may get constant knocks from trolleys or our elbows whenever you're trying to sleep. And don't get me started on 'ice and a slice'. You really won't want to know where that particular lemon was just before we put it in your drink.

ARE MOST OF THE MALE CABIN CREW MEMBERS GAY?

I don't know about 'most' of them. And Prince William can attest to a lot of them being straight – because his father-in-law Michael Middleton was cabin crew with British Airways in the 1970s when he met his wife Carole. She was cabin crew on the same airline – and like a surprising number of cabin crew he went on to train as a pilot.

As cabin crew author Jennie Jordan points out in her comedy novel, *Sky High*, some straight men deliberately choose to defy expectations by becoming cabin crew. 'I flew with one guy who tried to sleep with pretty much every woman he met. He certainly didn't want to spend his life surrounded by other straight men. So he became cabin crew knowing he'd have less competition for the women on his planes, and because he thought he could benefit from the advantage of surprise when he chatted all the women up. I decided to make him Matt, one of the characters in my novel,' she says.

Meanwhile, in her best-selling book, Cabin Fever, author Mandy Smith also writes about the Virgin boys who were so straight they had slept with almost every female member of almost every flight they took.

There are also lots of straight married couples in most crews – though being in a relationship with someone is no guarantee that you'll get to fly with them. Crew say long term relationships are hard enough to maintain if your other half will always be at home waiting for you. If he or she is always on another plane it's tougher still.

DO FEMALE CABIN CREW REALLY MARRY WEALTHIER THAN ANY OTHER WOMEN?

Lots of them certainly do pretty well. Russian president Vladimir Putin met his ex-wife Lyudmila when she used to fly for Aeroflot. They split after decades together – amid rumours that he'd salted away enough money to make him one of the richest men on the planet.

Hajah Mariam, meanwhile was crew with Royal Brunei Airlines in the 1970s when she met the Sultan of Brunei – who really was said to be the richest man in the world. They were married for 21 years – and their divorce is still said to be one of the most expensive in history.

Other famous former crew include the Queen of Sweden – and even Kim Kardashian's mum Kris Jenner. *Frasier* star Kelsey Grammer got chatting to British Airways flight attendant Kayte Walsh on a flight to the UK in 2009 – they've since got married and had three kids. Clint Eastward isn't far behind. He's got two kids with his former cabin crew wife.

Do male crew members fare as well? It's harder to say as they seem to keep it very quiet if they do. If anyone can think of any great examples let me know and I'll add them to an update of the book.

IS IT TRUE THAT PILOTS AND CO-PILOTS AREN'T ALLOWED TO EAT THE SAME MEAL, IN CASE THE FOOD HAS GONE OFF AND THEY GET SICK?

I think this story began after the 1980 disaster comedy film *Airplane!* when both pilots got sick and we got a shot of the two meals with identical tell-tale fish bones suggesting where the bug had come from.

In real life there are obviously very serious worries over contaminated food – for crew and passengers alike. I'm told that some airlines do ask their flight deck crew to each pick a different dish form the in-flight menu – but that's not the rule where I've flown. The captain and first officer and co tend to get a selection of special items, in a special part of the food cart, that they can choose from. But many just pick from the usual First or Business Class menu – so if you've paid a fortune to fly First and your choice isn't available that could be why.

ARE PILOTS ALLOWED TO WEAR GLASSES?

Yes, pilots don't need to have 20/20 vision to train and work on the flight deck. They will have to have their eyes and vision tested – at the start and regularly thereafter. If anyone on the flight deck does need glasses, they are required to carry a spare set at all times. Pilots are allowed to wear contact lenses as well and there are specific rules for polarised and photo-chromatic glasses that can be a little riskier as they cut the amount of light that goes through them.

Slightly worryingly, pilots can be colour blind and still fly a plane – though the exact rules vary around the world and depend on which colours a pilot can't see.

IS MY PLANE A RACIST?

Well, it's almost certainly white. And chances are that the one in front, behind, above and below you is white as well. But planes don't start that way. They normally look green, oddly enough, when they are first assembled at Boing or Airbus, before the coloured protective shields are peeled off them. But after that they tend to be painted white.

Urban legend says it's because of weight – that dark paint weighs more than white paint. But pilots say that's not true. The main reason airlines go for a mainly white look is heat. It reflects more light and heat, on the ground and up high, so it keeps planes cooler. Concorde actually needed special super-white paint as it got even hotter at its altitude and speed. Safety is another reason. At maintenance time it's easier to see cracks, dents, oil leaks or other hazards on a surface painted white. A largely white plane is more likely to be spotted in a search and rescue operation if the very worst happens. It's also easier for birds to see, so there's less danger of bird strikes.

Last of all, it's also better economics for airlines. Many trade their planes at some point – and a rival carrier is more likely to buy a white plane that needs less re-touching to re-emerge in a new livery.

DO CREWS GIVE PLANES A NICKNAME?

We don't. But planes get them. Every airline has a call-sign to identify it to air traffic control and others. It's not exactly the same as the flight number. The first British Airways flight of the day to Los Angeles is currently BA283. But this isn't how it's referred to by pilots or controllers. It is Speedbird, not BA, a name going right back to 1932.

The names are chosen to be clear in English, the international language of flight. And to be relatively distinct from each other. Before consolidation cleared a lot of US skies, many airlines had the word American in their name. But only the main AA got the American call-sign. The former American West was Cactus, for example.

Other airlines are obvious. Virgin Atlantic is Virgin, though Virgin America is Redwood. United is United. Air Lingus is Shamrock. And China Airlines is Dynasty. Planes also have registration details, like car licence plates. They'll be on the fuselage, which you may see as you board. And they will be on metal labels attached somewhere in most galleys and near emergency exits.

Apart from that, the 747 is often the Queen of the Skies. The 737 is the Workhorse. The autopilot is 'George' after the man who invented it, George DeBeeson. And Airbus is only called a Scarebus with affection.

WHAT'S THE BEST TIP CABIN CREW CAN GIVE TO FREQUENT FLIERS?

There's masses of advice. But I like this one – a sure fire way to make sure you don't leave something vital like your passport or money in your hotel safe. It's because of a trick we're taught in flight training.

If we're going to use a hotel safe (and managers tell crew to do so, especially for passports, layover cash, credit cards or other valuables if we're lucky enough to have any) then we put a single shoe in with them. And not just any shoe. We put one of our work shoes in the safe.

Sounds odd? Well if it's a shoe we use at work then we'll need it when we check out of the room as we head back to the airport. If we're all uniformed up but we don't have two shoes on our feet, then we remember to look in the safe for the missing one – and we don't leave our valuables for housekeeping to rifle through later in the day.

It's a trick anyone can use, even if you're not at work. Just decide which pair of shoes you're likely to wear to fly home in. Then put one of them in the safe with your valuables. A trainer is fine. A flip flop will do. But if you can't get out of the hotel with just one of them then it will be the perfect reminder to look in the safe.

A final word on this though. Remembering to empty a hotel safe is no good if you forget what the combination is. So make it easy. If a 4-digit code is required most crew use the PIN number for their credit or debit cards. If it's a 6-digit code then we'll probably use our date of birth. Managers tell us there's no reason to reinvent the wheel and come up with some new number for a hotel safe. Just put that travel shoe in there and nothing (hopefully) can go wrong.

CABIN CREW ARE ALL AIR-HEADS, RIGHT?

Try telling that to Johanna Siguroardottir, the longest standing Member of the Icelandic Parliament and the first female Prime Minister of her country. She was cabin crew for Iceland Air before entering politics and crashing all manner of glass ceilings.

Don't assume the crew just lie by the pool or go shopping on layovers. On almost every flight I do I meet people who run small businesses when they're not up in the air. Baking and cake making is big right now but there's always something new. The crew on your flight could be almost anything: personal trainers, life coaches, wedding planners, dog walkers, tour guides or photographers – you name it. I've flown with several people who volunteered as police officers on their days off, so when they weren't pouring people coffee they were arresting them.

Lots of crew are part-timers – and they have lots of irons in the fire on their rest days. Several of my friends are training to be pilots. Some are aiming to work in security or other airport-based functions. Others want to get into crew training or management. We're an ambitious bunch, by and large. We get plenty of time in overseas hotel rooms to plan our next careers. And most of us dream about being in First Class on our future flights – as passengers.

IF I ACCIDENTALLY LEAVE SOMETHING ON A PLANE WILL I GET IT BACK?

You'll get it back if you log on to eBay the following day. That's where crew sell everything we pick up as we walk through the plane after a long flight. And unfortunately that might not be a complete joke. Everything should get found on a plane, either by us or by the cleaners who swarm on the moment we leave. Security rules mean planes can't have any unattended or unauthorised items on them – security staff do test this by regularly leaving things hidden away on planes, just to see if they do in fact get spotted and removed by the appropriate people.

Anything genuinely left by a passenger should, of course, get logged and go to a Lost Property department – and they may want to know where you were sitting as part of the claims process so it's always worth holding on to your boarding pass.

That said, other things can happen, and that's another reason not to annoy your cabin crew. One old friend, possibly one of the nicest, kindest people I know, talks of a flight from hell with a huge extended family flying half in Business Class and half in other cheaper cabins. The Business Class contingent, where she was working, were rude from start to finish. So were the rest of the family who broke the rules and kept coming through the curtains to talk to them. She remembers the relief when they got back to London and the passengers headed away over the air bridge. And she remembers finding what looked like a brand new, cashmere, Hermes scarf in the overhead bin above where the rudest man of the lot had been sitting.

'If it had been left by any other passenger I would have handed it in. But because it was them I couldn't bring myself to do it. The scarf accidentally fell into my cabin bag and about four months later, when I felt safe, it accidentally got sold online. I only made about £40 but I felt I'd earned every penny,' she told me, still feeling guilty after all these years.

THE CREW ON MY FLIGHT SEEM TO BE GOOD FRIENDS. DO YOU FLY WITH THE SAME PEOPLE ALL THE TIME?

I'd have thought exactly the same when I first began to fly. The crews I looked at all seemed to be having a great time, they were laughing and smiling. It looked as if they were working with old friends. So I signed up. And then I learned the truth. The laughs and smiles aren't fake, as such. They're sort of put on, to get us through the flight and make time go faster.

On a Boeing 747 we fly at around 550 miles an hour and we make friends as supersonic speed as well. If you've just got one flight, and maybe a one day layover to get to know someone, you might as well cut to the chase. Aluminium tubes aren't good places for long, slow-burn conversations. So it's: 'You seeing someone? Single, married, gay, straight? Been doing this for a long time? Love it? Hate it? Friends on board? Enemies? Got any gossip? You been up front to see the size of the ring the lady's wearing in 4B?'

The one thing that sets crew friends apart from real friends is that we tend to be pretty bad at remembering names. When you fly with a different dozen every four days it's hard to keep up. That's why so many crew refer to both sexes, in all situations, as 'hon'. And it's not as if passengers use our names very often either (except when they want to complain about us). If you like cabin crew humour look for the cartoons from the endlessly clever Kelly Kincaid at JetLaggedComic.com. One of my favourites has a cabin manager making a welcome PA on the mic saying: 'Ladies and Gentlemen, welcome aboard! My name is Hey You! and today I have the pleasure of working with Excuse Me! And Oh Miss!'

WHY DO CABIN CREW SPILL DRINKS?

It's not because they're clumsy. It's not because of turbulence. It's not because they're doing tough jobs in tiny spaces. No. In most cases cabin crew spill drinks because they want to. We pour drinks every day, after all. Hundreds of them on every single flight we do.

We pour hot drinks, cold drinks, expensive drinks, the lot. So we get pretty good at it. So if we do spill them, take a look at who we spill them on. Chances are it won't be the lovely, polite little old lady in 16B. Or the super-hot passenger with the beautiful eyes in 34F. No, it's far more likely to be the irritating man who complained rudely about the delays at boarding and hasn't let up since. Or it might be the super-demanding woman who pressed her call button four times in the first half hour of the flight. Coincidence? I couldn't possibly say.

WHAT'S THE FIRST THING CABIN CREW DO WHEN THEY GET TO A LAYOVER HOTEL?

Ditch the uniform, have a shower and grab a drink? Those are pretty good guesses. But there are a few other things we're told about in training that I recommend to family and friends when they travel. First up? Look for the nearest emergency stairs – it's just like looking for the nearest emergency exit on the plane. There should be a diagram on the back of your hotel door – but take thirty seconds to check it out in reality as well. Then repeat it in your head, so it sticks. 'Turn left outside my door. Go seven doors down. It's on the Right.' If the hotel corridors are dark and full of smoke then this knowledge can save you.

On that note, a bit of fire awareness never goes amiss anyway. We're trained to remember to touch our room doors before opening them in a fire. If they're hot then the fire could be right outside, and you can face blowback if you open it fast or at all. If there are hazards and you can't get to the emergency exit then we're told to fill the bath, put wet towels under the door to stop smoke coming through and to stay low where the air is easier to breathe. We're told to turn off the air-conditioning – it can bring smoke or even fire into the room – and to try to find a sheet or some other signal to tell those outside that we are trapped.

There's one other thing some of us do in a new hotel room – or indeed every time we go back to our hotel room. We pull back the shower curtain, open the wardrobes and have a quick look on to the balcony. Some crew actually look under their beds as well. Statistically there really isn't going to be a dangerous stranger lurking in or around your hotel room. But if you're there to relax you might as well get some peace of mind and make sure.

A final safety tip, especially for people travelling alone, is to at least give a few clues about our movements. At crew training we're told that some people leave notes in their hotel rooms to say where they're going and when. If something happens, and the authorities find a note saying: 'Thursday at 4pm. Leaving to wander round the mall and then get a burger' then it could help them investigate exactly where we might be and what's happened to us.

On a lighter note, there's an old cabin crew saying. How do you know which rooms in a hotel have got airline crew in them? They're the ones with the 'Do Not Disturb' signs on the doors all day. Most of us put them on there the moment we arrive. We're there to rest. Experience tells us that hotel housekeeping works to strange timetables, just like we do. So there's no guarantee that chambermaids, maintenance staff or others will only arrive in the morning. If you need a nap, you need that sign on your door.

WHAT KIND OF THINGS DO CREW GET UP TO IN LAYOVER HOTELS? IS IT PARTY TIME, LIKE A WEEK LONG HOLIDAY?

Is it like a week long holiday? The days of staying almost anywhere for a week are long gone. If you think the golden age of travel has ended for passengers then you'll be horrified how bad it is for crew. A long-haul transatlantic or transcontinental flight is likely to include just one night in a hotel. If you fly west on a Monday morning and arrive Monday afternoon (which can include a twelve hour flight, because of the time changes along the way) you may well just get that one night in the layover hotel. You'll check out on Tuesday afternoon and be on the Tuesday night red-eye heading east back to base and arriving early on Wednesday morning. After a single full day off on the Thursday you'll be back in the air to do it all again on the Friday. And so it goes on.

If you want to learn a bit more about the reality of crew life, then my old friend Jennie Jordan made me laugh when she described all the fun, confusion (and naughtiness) of her first ever layover in her great book, *Flying High*. Others have been open-mouthed at how the outrageous former Virgin Atlantic cabin crew member Mandy Smith describes the same (even wilder) events in her best-seller *Cabin Pressure*.

But one thing carries more weight than all this. Nowadays, with tight schedules, fast turnarounds and ever increasing passenger demand there's one thing cabin crew want to do the most on a layover. We want to sleep.

IS EVERY AIRLINE EMPLOYEE IN THE MILE HIGH CLUB? AND HOW CAN PASSENGERS JOIN?

I thought I'd leave this one to last. The mile high club has always obsessed people – but does it really exist? Of course it does. You can't expect people not to try something that gets talked about all the time. Famous names who've done it, so they say, include model Miranda Kerr and ex-husband Orlando Bloom. There's Chris Brown and Kris Jennner (not together) and Janet Jackson. Carmen Electra even talks about the 'special knock' she and ex-husband Dave Navarro worked out so she would know it was him outside the toilet door when they did the deed.

As for the rest of us, maybe you can't blame people for trying to find some way to pass the time on a seemingly endless long haul flight.

But if I'm honest, far more people talk about the mile high club than actually join it. From a crew point of view there are several reasons to steer clear. If we're caught acting badly in uniform (or even half-in uniform) we can get sacked. Plus most of the time we're too exhausted. Plus if we fancy a fellow crew member we're probably on the way to a nice layover hotel where we can have a lot more fun. And if we fancy a passenger we'd probably prefer their number so we can at least get dinner off them as well.

So while it can seem like a rite of passage it's far from compulsory.

And joining up isn't actually as easy as it seems. If you're on a flight right now then look around. If you're in economy you'll be surrounded by dozens of people – more than 100 in most rear cabins. You'll have a minimum of two crew on duty in the galley (whose job is to go into the toilets to do a quick 'brush and flush' at least twice an hour) and depending on the plane layout you'll have people looking right at (or sitting right alongside, poor people) the lavatory door.

Then there's the lav itself. It's not the most romantic of places. It's not the biggest of places either.

So if you're going to join the club it's probably best to be flying Business Class – better, in fact, than flying in First. That's because First is normally where the door to the Flight Deck can be found. That door has to be policed really well – cabin crew have to be around it at all times. It's also got a camera above it, so the pilot and team can see what is going on outside.

The more lavish private 'cabins' in Business and First Class on new planes may look a good spot for some fun. Especially when the marketing drops little hints about the double beds you can form in adjoining pods. But remember the doors and walls around the pods don't go up to the ceiling. They have to be low enough for cabin crew to look over for safety reasons. So you're still on show.

The larger toilets in First may make the whole thing more attractive. As can the extraordinary shower rooms on the likes of Emirates where signs apparently say 'maximum two occupants'. Why two occupants, Emirates has been asked. In case a second passenger needs assistance, it responded. 'And of course it depends on how you define assistance,' as my friend at www.OneMileAtATime.com says.

Finally, if you really must try this, then timing is everything. The worst times are at the start or end of flights, when cabin crew are at their busiest, when none of them are on breaks, when most passengers are awake and when trolleys are being pushed up and down the aisles. The 'best' times will be mid-flight, when the lights are low, plenty of people are dozing and the back of the plane can be a lonely place. But as you head back there, do just take a look at all the people covered in blankets in the back row of economy. Who really knows what's going on back there in the dead of night?

HAVE YOU TOLD US ABSOLUTELY EVERYTHING IN THIS BOOK?

I'll be honest and say no. Some things might have just slipped my mind, or not even have occurred to me – that's why I'm on Twitter @WelcomeFlyer - if you've got extra issues you'd like me to raise when I update the book then do just let me know there. Things change, of course, and new subjects and questions arise, so I may not have had the chance to write about all of those just yet.

And then there's the safety and the security aspect. Cabin crew training does involve a lot of information about emergencies, terrorism, hijacking and other horrors. I've thought long and hard about this information. I'm so pleased I know it – and that all the crews I fly with know it. But I simply don't believe it should be passed out, WikiLeaks fashion, to the world at large. Airlines, airports and everyone connected to them want us all to be safe. We need some secret procedures that we can swing into action if the worst happens – we need some code words and phrases that tell us something out of the ordinary is going on – and to suggest how we deal with it. None of this will be effective if the bad guys know exactly what all this stuff is in advance. I'm not over-blowing my role here. The bad guys probably know all this already – they won't need a fun little book from me to explain it all. But I still feel a responsibility to keep some trade secrets so that's what I've done.

But that's not the way I want this book to end. I don't want it to close on a down. Flying is safe – and despite the stresses, strains and cutbacks it can still be a whole lot of fun. I look up and down my cabins when I fly and I think: these people may be heading off to, or coming back from, a dream holiday. Or they're excited about some business trip and a great new opportunity. This is a big deal. Lots of my Twitter crew colleagues talk about 'bringing back the glamour' of flight. That's probably not going to happen. But flying is still an amazing adventure. I still love it. So one more time – happy travels. Wear your seatbelt, pay attention to the safety demo, smile at your crew – and Welcome Aboard!